SYSTEMIC CHANGE AND STABILIZATION IN EASTERN EUROPE

Systemic Change and Stabilization in Eastern Europe

Edited by

László CSABA

With contributions by Anders Aslund, Paul Dembinski, Raimund
Dietz, Grzegorz Kolodko, Jacques Morriset, Gábor Oblath,
Gérard Roland and Iván Szegvári

Dartmouth

Aldershot · Brookfield USA · Hong Kong · Singapore · Sydney

Published by
Dartmouth Publishing Company Limited
Gower House, Croft Road
Aldershot, Hants GU11 3HR
England

Dartmouth Publishing Company
Old Post Road
Brookfield, Vermont 05036
USA

A CIP catalogue record for this book is available from the British Library and the US Library of Congress.

Printed in Great Britain by
Billing & Sons Ltd, Worcester

ISBN 1 85521 204 8

Contents

Foreword

This volume has been called into being by the growing international interest in affairs of systemic transformation and economic stabilization in what used to be termed 'Eastern Europe' in the political parlance of the post-Yalta period. After the collapse of the state socialist systems, it is the very standards of evaluation which have undergone a fundamental change. The questions arising in the many ways unexpected developments are more numerous, than are answers. With the post-revolutionary emphasis over and under the shadows of the new oil price instability, triggered by the Gulf crisis, and experiencing the serious repercussions of a collapsing Soviet empire, the countries of Central and Southeastern Europe face a protracted and painful transition from Soviet socialism to a liberal political and economic order. It is a historically unprecedented challenge to these nations, and those who fail to address the underlying economic issues, will face a historical decay, a long term degeneration into the underdeveloped world. From the debtors' prison there is no European perspective for the coming generations, but the prospect of commonalty with the much too well known, tragic fate of stagnating nations around the globe. In the meantime, the experience of newly industrializing countries may also illustrate: the modern world is not governed by historic predetermination. Nations who used to be hardly mentioned in the 40s or 50s are becoming world champs in many walks of life. In a nutshell, even abstracting from the dangers of a Soviet civil war waged by nuclear weapons, there's a lot of interesting things for the outside world as well to follow in the unique laboratory of the other half of the European continent.

What are the roots and driving forces, motivations and tricks of successful versus unsuccessful adjustment and transition strategies? This comprehensive field of research is in the focus of activities of the European Association for Comparative Economic Studies, whose first international conference, held in Verona (Italy) between 27-29 Sept., 1990 gave the impetus to the authors to present the first draft of their papers. Out of the more than 150 scientific presentations the editor selected eight outstanding contributions which may provide some insight into the key issues of economic stabilization and systemic transition to capitalism. The outcome might be of lasting interest for students of comparative systems, of economic policies, of international relations, as well as for bankers, journalists and policymakers alike. I should also like to take this opportunity and thank the organizers of the Verona gathering, Prof. Sylvana Malle, then President of the Italian Association for the Study of Comparative Economic Systems and Dr. Carlo Frateschi, Senior Fellow at the University of Padua for enabling us the lively exchange of ideas, which has lead each author of this book to revise, update, restructure and generally improve the standards of his study.

Budapest, 15 February 1991.

László Csaba
Vice-President of EACES

Part I
Introduction

1 New perspectives on systemic change and stabilization in Central Europe: an overview

by László Csaba

The turn of the 1980s/1990s has surely been one of the most fascinating periods of modern European history. With the collapse of state socialism in Eastern Europe and the disintegrating Soviet empire small nations in Central and Southeastern Europe have been facing unexpected challenges. Instead of cautiously or radically reforming the socialist economy they could opt for Western order: the pluralistic political and economic structures.

The objective is not subject to discussion among the major policy forming forces in any of these countries. It is hotly debated, however, how, through which way and in what time horizon this target is to be attained. Not only the normal controversies of mature democracies emerged. The debate has been complicated by two peculiar aspects:

a   previously available evidence/knowledge of the planned economy and of comparative systems theory quickly depreciated as its subject matter simply disappeared. Thus established science in the East and Sovietology in the West could offer a limited help only.

b   Economic science in the West, especially mainstream economics operates with models, categories, motives and laws whose validity is (historically) conditioned by a fully fledged market order, that has evolved over the last three centuries. The fundamentals of this very system, however, have been annihilated in East and Central Europe by the expropriation of the expropriators four-five decades ago. Prolonged existence under a command system has

3

significantly modified (crippled) the behaviour of all economic agents including the private sector and households.

This is not the place to elaborate on what way distortional effects worked (Winiecki, J., 1988; Kornai, J- 1980; Csaba, L., 1990/a; Soós K. A., 1986). Let it suffice to note that this makes the Central European starting point fundamentally different from that of the privatization drive which has swept through many of the developed and developing nations during the 1980s. The story in Central and Southeastern Europe is not about expanding an already dominant private sector and cutting back an overextended state. It is about creating - and letting to evolve - the market order, where bureaucratic coordination is subordinate to market coordination. These terms of János Kornai (1984) are of crucial importance, as they imply a fundamental distinction from conventional wisdom, having classified the region's economies as 'centrally planned'. Planning - at least in the 1970s and 1980s - was practically nothing more than a ritual point of reference, and the lack of efficient central regulation (both in form of macroeconomic policies and of system design) has been one of the most conspicuous features in the second half of the 1980s, contributing directly to the collapse of state socialism.

The abolition of central planning thus has taken place well before the dissolution of its agency in Hungary (a step still to be taken in other Central European democracies). However, monetary and market regulation could not take over, as they continued to remain subordinate to bureaucratic bargains. Thus it is the uncontrolled and in many ways spontaneous intra-bureaucratic power game which shapes actual decisions and outcomes, not officially promulgated general rules, governmental policies or other declarations of intent. This state of art seem to have survived the political earthquake - which is not quite unparalleled in European history. In other words, disintegration and the inability to implement governmental priorities is one of the worst legacies of the ancien régime. Thus the task faced by new democracies is historically unprecedented. On the one hand they have to create what is for Western privatization policies given: a middle class and authentic agents of the market economy. On the other hand, they need to reregulate as well: in part by abolishing the old and creating a small but efficient new governmental administration, in part by bringing about the frame in which the expansion of the private sector is both faster and socially more accepted than under fully spontaneous (wild West type of) evolution.

In other words a new field of scientific analysis has been created by the historic challenges. Meanwhile governmental agencies are forced to act by political exigencies much earlier than ready made recipes were available. Therefore a fruitful and continuous interaction of policymakers and researchers has come into being producing a large number of advisory committees, international conferences and also legislation forming the empirical material in much different directions than any field of the economics profession would have

4

forecasted five or ten years ago.

In the enjoyably wide and controversial source material this book intends to be something peculiar. International organizations, especially the IMF, the World Bank and the OECD have convened several international conferences on the problems of transition to the market, often resulting in books. These address mostly the general theory of systemic transformation - well exemplified by a provocative title of Rüdiger Dornbusch from the 28-30 November 1990 OECD seminar: 'How to create a market economy in seven days?' General issues are neatly summarized in an already published other conference volume of the OECD. (Blommestein, H. - Marrese, M. - Zecchini, S., eds. 1991). Mention should be made of the European Communities, which sponsors a decade of annual research conferences of the European Science Foundation on the subject. Country studies also proliferate, partly in the countries themselves, capitalizing on the symbiosis of new intellectual freedoms with new material hardships.

There is neither general theory nor country specific analysis in this volume. What is being attempted is to produce an applied and comparative theory of systemic change. We've got the advantage of the authors' being connected by an all-European intellectual stream of the network of EACES. We've got the advantage of having an experience of many years of observation of reforms under one party rule as well as of a year of shock therapy in Poland and in Yugoslavia. Thus we might be able to make the first distinctions among more or less relevant propositions and theoretical statements. For instance, supporters of the big bang approach have concluded on the base of data for the first quarter that the phase of corrective inflation in Poland were over (Lipton and Sachs, 1990). Knowing that annual rates of inflation both in Poland and Yugoslavia remained well into the triple digit margin, this proposition - its theoretical fineness notwithstanding - does not sound particularly convincing from the policy point of view. Similarly, previous Czech propositions about their ability of managing systemic and structural change without sizable inflation (Klaus, 1990) sound like a myth when one reads (without much surprise) about official estimates of 30 per cent inflation for 1991, the first actual year of Czecho-Slovak reforms (Die CSFR.. 1991).

What used to be an independent East German state provides the observer with ample illustration about the costs and benefits of a jump into the market. On the one hand it could be proven (Siebert, H. 1990) that for the Federal Republic swallowing an economy which is one tenth of its own is no problem whatsoever. On the other hand, with the time passing it turned out that official forecasts of the costs of integration are heavily biased downwards (from the Western perspective). Meanwhile the pains to those being swallowed are also well above previous expectations. In what's undoubtedly a beneficial process in the long run (and was a political must, as retroactively demonstrated by events in the Baltic states and Russia in January 1991), the ex offico optimistic Treuhandanstalt forecasted a 70 per cent closure rate for the previous GDR industry with 1,3 Mn open unemployed and 1,7 Mn part time workers from among a 9 Mn strong labour force despite a mushrooming private sector (cf Handelsblatt, 19 Dec. 1990. and Neue Zürcher Zeitung 11 Jan., 1991).

We try to take stock of this empirical evidence just as much as the sobering experiences with ill-concieved particularistic and gradualist attempts. It seems to the present author, that factors usually outside the scope of attention of standard economics may have to be given their proper role. Continuity both in stock variables, and in behavioural norms of economic agents, of masses of people, social expectations, national peculiarities and the historic legacy may milden much of the radicality in any new governments's endavour. This might explain why such a wide variety of 'extraeconomic constraints' produce similar results in thwarting theoretically clear propositions of mainstream economics, if applied indiscriminately.

There's widespread agreement among the contributors to the present volume, that opening up the institutionally closed postsocialist economies and liberalizing the foreign trade regime as well as of the inflow of foreign direct investment is of paramount importance in the final success of the entire exercise. Though views somewhat differ over the proper timing of the measures pertaining to the foreign economic sector, nobody believes that any of the economies in question could be stabilized without substantial liberalization. This consensus may stem from the authors' all being citizens of small or medium sized countries as well as our explicit rejection of dealing with the Soviet economy. This is not to propose that citizens of what's today the Soviet Federation may not draw on the experience collected here, if and when they intend to implement systemic change, i.e. transform rather than improve state socialism. Still, for the present subject the Soviet Union is treated only as an important element of the external environment surrounding the countries transforming their economic order. Other technicalities as well as strategic issues in opening up these economies may easily be omitted from this volume, as a currently published compendium of papers by internationally established scholars (Köves, A. - Marer, P. eds., 1991) provides an exhaustive elaboration of these. Sharing their major conclusions this volume intentionally, focuses on domestic aspects of systemic change and its role in achieving the longer term stabilization of the Central European economies.

The Southeast European countries are by and large not included in the volume, as - at the time of writing - none of them have yet left firmly behind the stage of a single force dominating the political scene. It is obviously true in Romania and applies increasingly to Serbia, having a say through the federal army also in other constituents of Yugoslavia, whereas Bulgaria and Albania haven't crossed the Rubicon formally either.

Having delineated the subject, let us have a brief overview of the outcome. The structure of the present volume goes as follows. In Part Two substantive issues of systemic change are discussed, which - according to the consensus view - form the final objective of the

6

exercise: an economy based on predominantly private property and on currency convertibility. Chapter Two is devoted thus to privatization, i.e. to the core of the problem through discussing ways and programs to achieve the end, whereas Chapter Three gives an overview of the actual 'state of art' as reflected synthetically in the degree of convertibility of the national currencies of the reforming countries. In Part Three theoretical and policy issues are surveyed, i.e. ways and means to attain the target formulated in the previous Part. How to privatize and how not, how to stabilize and how not, what is the correct sequence of the measures to be taken? Although authors of the various Chapters come to somewhat different conclusions, none of them share the fashionable view that the debate on sequencing were a loss of time enabling vested interest to sabotage systemic change. (Schrettl, W. 1991). Empirical evidence of the Central European countries caution against the indiscriminate adoption of quick fixes readily offered by some quarters of the academic establishment. In Part Four external conditions i.e. the environment of stabilization and the transition are discussed. The collapse of the formerly predominant Comecon environment of state trading poses a rarely discussed peculiar challenge for the Central European states. On the other hand the West also has a role to play in bringing about that systemic congruity which might enable the postsocialist countries of Central Europe to be integrated into the Single European Market by the turn of the millennium.

After the abortive Shatalin Plan I don't see much chance for any all-Soviet attempt to introduce the market order across the board in the whole present federation. However under a new political constellation, Russian, Baltic or Caucasian reformers or even governments of some developing country with a strong étatiste tradition may well want the face the issue of transforming their whole system into the market. They may capitalize primarily on Part Two devoted to the most general and politically most sexy issues of systemic change: privatization and convertibility.

Privatization has had very little policy relevant literature up until recent years. Theory was mostly confined to proving the superiority (or inferiority) of private firms over public companies. Policy steps in this area - except for Chile - tended to be minor as they haven't changed the basic macroeconomic pattern of ownership.

In some cases privatization was a success story, in others much less so (depending on the contestability of the given market and on the nature of the given activity). With the fall of state socialism previous conservative experimentation gained immediate policy relevance shaping the entire strategies of the new national governments. In his chapter Anders Aslund provides a very useful summary of internationally available privatization evidence and makes several propositions on how the relevant options can be applied in Central and Eastern Europe. His empirical reference base is mostly Poland, thus counterbalancing Hungarian overrepresentation among the contributions. His appeal for a quick privatization is one of the fundamental messages of his study. He lists several arguments proving why privatization should not be subordinate to fiscal considerations, as in this case the process becomes so protracted, that the overall improvement in macroeconomic efficiency might remain negligible. He also contests the fashionable view that first agriculture should be privatized. Given the agricultural overemployment in all postsocialist states and the secularly depressed (international) prices for farm products a quick privatization may result in disproportionate rural unemployment. This leads to his unambiguous stance against restitution as a basic method to create proprietors: by opening this gate a decade of legal disputes and uncertainties is being created that may undercut the whole transition. He also argues for a free distribution of - at least a part - of state property in order to create a point of no return and a sizable initial momentum for the new capitalist class.

If Aslund approaches to the issue 'from above', i.e. from the perspective of system design, Szegvári on convertibility adopts the perspective 'from below'. In his down-to-earth study he raises the question why the once much heralded liberalizing steps in fact produced rather destabilization of their unchanged overall environment than its gradual change towards the market. Similarly to Kolodko (writing in Chapter 7) he thinks that tasks of macro economic stabilization and systemic change often imply more contradictory than complementary tasks. The virtue of this paper is a comparative study of empirical evidence. On this base he is rather skeptical on the sustainability of currency convertibility before the Central European states and Yugoslavia had mastered their structural crisis. By overviewing the role of foreign exchange accounts and of the paradoxes of restrictive monetary policies applied in an environment where bankruptcy is truly exceptional he points to the fragility of the newly won convertibility of the zloty, the forint and the dinar. By presenting his reservations as bluntly as Aslund argues for his optimistic version Szegvári represents the other end of the spectrum of voices permanently influencing policymakers in the economies under transition.

Part Three of the book is on the theory and policy of how to move from the depressing present to the bright future. This entails questions of what to do, why to do, what way to do and in what sequence to do the right thing. Being on the borderline of economics and politics the Walloon contributor calls it the political economy problems of the transition.

In Chapter Five Roland addresses a core problem of what he terms 'sequencing tactics', i.e. ways to overcome the inevitable rightist-populist backlash at the first bites of the transition. He produces an applied economic theory framework for the uncharted waters of systemic transformation which avoids being country specific. Using the theory of collective action he focuses on the (changing) preferences of the individual in explaining those massive changes of sides without which social change could never (have) take(n) those historic dimensions which have fundamentally restructured the state socialist socioeconomic setup. His description of the state socialist

8

inequalities call strongly into a question the fashionable theories (e.g. Kornai, 1988, and Hewett, 1988) portraying the 'equality versus efficiency' issue being the crux of the (social side of) the problem. As Roland proves, it is rather the redistribution of previous privileges (situation rents) that explains social resistance to marketization. It is the priorities of the least rather than the best informed which matters as the former tend to change their views the most. Whereas stabilization should occur in one leap, systemic transformation should follow a sequencing tactics with sizable 'carrots' at initial stages for numerous interest groups. Roland votes for the 'first privatize, than liberalize' sequencing. Bankruptcies - he notes - especially in the state sector can hardly be expected in the early stage of systemic change, as this is the core of macroeconomic restructuring, which is - after all - the last phase in the sequence Roland proposes. Free distribution schemes of privatization in his view would probably end up with similar scandal-ridden cases as 'spontaneous', 'wild' or nomenklatura privatization did in Poland (Nuti, 1991) and Hungary (Csaba, 1990/b and Newberry, 1991) - ending up in a rightist populist backlash, thus giving a flaw to the entire process. Therefore reliance on foreign direct investments on the one hand, and the foreign investors' behaving as agents of civilized rather than cowboy capitalism should be the two sides of the same coin. Roland's paper is probably the best example of what may be termed 'radical gradualism', forming the backbone of this volume. Roland addresses the interest structures resisting marketization in a multidisciplinary perspective and finds those being much more intricate than conventionally postulated, therefore more elaborate policies - such as selective rather than automatic across-the-board bankruptcies are needed to provide momentum for systemic change. Sequencing in his view implies the broad ranking of transition phases according to political expediency simultaneously preserving basic economic congruity of the measures promoting the evolution of a market order. However of the minimal speed and quantity requirements proper account should be taken.

Chapter Six, written by Dembinski and Morriset is on outcomes of IMF stabilization policies in Latin America and in Eastern Europe in a comparative perspective. Their basic message cast doubt over the suitability of conventional stabilization policies to produce those acceptable growth rates which external lenders expect from adjustment in indebted nations. Their fundamental idea is that the coat tailored to par excellence cyclical imbalances do not suit to the figure of structural and growth-disequilibria. Credit contraction may not result in current account surpluses or (even less) in the reduction of the rate of inflation. By presenting a formalized approach they lend extra support to their critical stance. Credit contraction is bound to slow down adjustment and harm output levels - this is what they prove, further it may even worsen inflation. Their basic policy recommendation is to revert standard propositions for sequencing, and make structural and systemic treatment preceding (conventional) stabilization measures.

In his essay Kolodko addresses a peculiar issue in Chapter Seven:

the responsibility of theorists turned into policymakers and/or their closest advisors. Since state socialism collapsed in all walks of life, the room is open to experiment with any radical idea. He rejects both the previously prevailing self-limiting empiricism as well as the recently fashionable arrogant messianism of various wizards allegedly possessing with the single best solution to all dilemmas. Kolodko warns of the rather widespread mistake of mixing up abstract models with socio-political exigencies emerging in a multi-faceted crisis and transformation period. The need to act may emerge earlier then truly scientific answers are available, still this does not exempt policymakers of the consequences of their ignorance: predominant governmental improvisations imply a fairly suboptimal use of commonly available evidence. Thus openly declared pragmatism of some governments were equally misguided and disastrous as the theoretical obsessions of others. He lays great emphasis on the specific contradictions stemming from the transitory nature of empirically observable economic regimes, carrying a heavy historical legacy under the new target-setting as well. Unlike Dembinski and Morriset, he favours the more conventional approach: first to stabilize and only later to change the fundamentals of the system. He gives a general frame of explanation why negative adjustment prevails and positive supply responses remain weak under shock therapy - ending up where Szegvári and the Dembinski-Morriset duo does with their different lines of thought. His invoking evidence of Latin American stabilization policies adds the empirical material to support the formalized argumentation of the Swiss contributors. Economists thus bear a crucial responsibility, whether or not they can visualize what brand of market economy are they actually bringing about in the postsocialist context of middle income countries. An overdose of monetarism may aggravate the already serious developmental drawbacks of Central Europe.

In Chapter Eight Oblath deals with a peculiar problem which remains often outside the focus of attention on systemic change: the legacy of the collapsing Comecon. Since trade with the Soviet Union used to be of dominant significance for economic policies all over the four decades of state socialism, both reorientation of commercial relations and the fundamental modification of the previous state trading system constitute shocks to the existing macroeconomic structures.

In this field the customary overpoliticization of issues diverted attention from processes actually taking place. For instance the Mazowiecki Government followed a tough principal stand in its talks vis-a-vis the Soviets insisting on (Sachs inspired) debt reduction or even on forgiving - on historic grounds - all or most of the 5,6 bn roubles Polish debt to the Soviet Union. In the meantime during 1990, i.e. a single year a surplus of 4,7 bn roubles appeared on the Polish current account. In other words most of the debt is already paid for, without any formal intergovernmental agreement. It is correct to note (Mizsei, 1990; and Winiecki, 1990, pp. 780-781) that this surplus is surely to blame for accelerating inflation (which seem

10

to have taken some IMF people by surprise). Equally unexpectedly, the Soviet share in Hungarian trade was cut by half between 1988 and 1990 without producing more than 2 per cent unemployment. The much feared series of bankruptcies haven't happened and Hungarian liquidity position in trade with the West even improved (Csaba, 1991).[1] So while theorists went out their way to prove the infeasibility of the whole exercise, the lion's share of the entire operation has been mastered, without sizable (extra) external help, without having recourse to rescheduling, debt relief or even special balance of payments credit facilities.

Under these circumstances it is of particular interest to see how technically the switchover from clearing to hard currency trade occurred, what kind of regulatory dilemmas and options emerged in the course of decisionmaking. The first hand experience of Oblath allows him to present an insightful paper to this 'terra incognita' as (for obvious reasons) no public description of the existing trade and payments regime has ever been presented to the English speaking community. His analysis is a valuable contribution to the realistic assessment of actual costs of a fundamental change in the trade regime entails for an economy which is already farther on the way of transforming its economic system than other Central European countries are (Csaba, 1990/b).

The contribution of Dietz is devoted to the role played by the other - quickly growing - half of the foreign economic intercourse on Central European systemic change, i.e. on relations with the West. Adopting a system theorists' approach the Austrian author deals with the ways and means, as well as the policies required for a post-socialist economy to become successful in its marketization. In other words, the issue is how to create systemic congruity between the domestic systems (shaped by the state socialist legacy) and the determinant external environment of the Single European Market? Only if the postsocialist systems obtain those fundamental characteristics that enable them to be integrated to the modern international economy, do they stand a chance for being integrated to the EC. On the other hand, Western countries can't simply wait and see if and when systemic transformation and economic stabilization succeeds, and decide only later, on this condition, their assistance to, and the possible integration of, (at least some of) the economies in transition. Economic processes may well tend to develop towards chaos rather than a liberal economic order unless well-founded competent and selective Western help is provided to mastering the historic task of transforming a command system into a liberal market order. Falling short of this task the Western countries will inevitably experience what they fear most: the uncontrolled spillover of the waves of a protracted crisis in Central and East Europe.

What are the conclusions - if any - to be drawn from such a multivocal choir of voices? Certainly everybody has the liberty to interpret these analyses according to his preferences. In my view however some tentative policy conclusions may well be drawn.

For the Central but also for the Southeast European economies,

11

and let me add - this time without elaboration - also for the Soviet economy and its components the actual task they face is to introduce a fully fledged market economy, with its appropriate private property structure and the rule of law (Rechtstaatlichkeit). Thus there's nothing more remote from reality than the assumption: 'The conceptual challenge they face is to structure a new order, one that absorbs the most beneficial institutions of capitalism into a socialist value system' (Feige, 1990, p. 2.) or that they were to resolve class conflicts via popular capitalism (ibidem, pp. 47-48). On the contrary, the theoretical debate may well (and surely will) go on, but in political terms it is over. It has become part and parcel of the political consensus in Eastern Europe (and of the professional consensus in the Soviet Union): the third way is not a feasible alternative to consider.[2] So if there is a danger, it is posed by the much too indiscriminate acceptance of conservative values in Central Europe and also in Russia, without paying sufficient attention to the social component making modern Western societies 'capitalism with a human face'. Due to the protracted nature of the crisis and the considerable time horizon of improvement, under socially insensitive technocratic practices the amount of social explosive may accumulate. Thus the general atmosphere of 'no more experimentation, please' dominating the East European region is good news and bad news in the same time. Good news, as long socialist grand designs are out of the political agenda for many years to come. Meanwhile European postsocialist societies are already intensively intertwined with advanced Western welfare states whose practices are widely known and appreciated by the Central and East European public. Due to the resultant social preferences these states are probably ill suited to become experimental fields for empirically yet untested radical monetarist economic propositions. The social feasibility of applicable economic theories may not be directly related to their intellectual appeal or fashionability.[3] This is the bad news.

What is needed thus is a kind of ordnungspolitisches Denken or radical gradualism. It implies that being conscious of the current state of art (i.e. the economic system's being an instable mixture of various constituting elements) governments do not justify or accept it. Rather they do have a clear objective they well as a blueprint about how to get to the land of promise. Moreover - they use their legitimacy to dose the medicine in sufficiently large packages. Only if the public is convinced that there's absolutely no other way, the government knows where it is driving to and how, and the public gives credence to the governmental programme, may radical changes be implemented (Millar, 1990 pp. 68-69) - this point is supported both by the relative success of Polish and the undoubted failure of Soviet attempts to marketize and stabilize in 1990.

A further conclusion from the limited knowledge available at this point is that the abstract theoretical and political debate on shock therapy may sidetrack energies from vital tasks. Most of the issues related to sequencing sounds quite different under Hungarian or Soviet, Bulgarian or East German conditions. Thus - as Winiecki (1990

12

p. 787-788) suggests, a country by country approach seems to be the justified in addressing all issues of the transition - just like in medicine it makes no sense to theorize about the vices and virtues of amputation per se. Similarly to this author the rapporteurs of the OECD volume, Blommestein, Marrese and Zecchini (1991, p. 20) have also found the theoretical debate being stronger than differences in actual policy advises of serious economists.

The limited but undoubted success of the changes in 1990 allow for giving up the illusions of swift systemic changes. True, systemic change and stabilization are intimately intertwined, but far from identical tasks. The former can be done quickly, the shortage economy is relatively easy to master, and hyperinflation can also be arrested. However as Balcerowicz (1991) noted, it does take years to create such fundamental institutions of the liberal order as capital market, labour market, constitutionally guaranteed proprietary rights as well as limiting the direct influence of organized minorities on policymaking. An other former theoretical supporter of quick fixes, Czech Privatization Minister Jezek now also believes that the operation will last three years at least. (Die CSFR...1991). This is the horizon in which the State Property Agency intends to complete in Hungary privatization of half of all public assets, with 130 privatizations already completed in the first 9 months of its existence (Csepi, 1991). And this is where is difference remains largely semantic between 'radical gradualism' and the 'jump into the market'.

We have learned a bit more about the dead ends of privatization. For one, transforming state owned firms into joint stock companies, which is normally seen as a welcome first step to their sale, have in fact turned out to be the most efficient way of nomenklatura privatization. The modern legal form has thus become an immediate barrier to actual transfer of state assets to private hands. In Hungary e.g. out of the more than 40 thousand restaurants and retail shops less than a fifth can, even in theory be privatized, as all the rest are already integral parts of various joint stock companies formed by the previous medium level control organs. This was one of the causes why the first privatization program simply faded away in a few months, just as public property did.

It seems to have become obvious in Hungary at least that restitution is bad economics. The presence of a single issue agrarian party pushing reprivatization of land has created continuous legal uncertainty, and slowed down the whole transformation process tremendously, as noone will ever invest until countless 'previous owners' may knock on the door. Moreover, restitution through vouchers (probably entitlements) is obviously inflationary. Moreover, as the chairman of the board of the Budapest stock exchange Bokros (1991) demonstrated, the high probability of cashing the vouchers (by the mostly elderly peasants) is bound to depress the entire securities' market and drive further up interest rates, thereby further aggravating economic recession, which will certainly last for some time during structural readjustment. Fundamental remains, however the standing legal uncertainty around once acquired property, which is hard to eschew once historic damages start to be undone, which undermines the entire economic order based on private property and freedom/sanctity of contract.

All in all, a lot of further research remains to be done before an empirically based and methodologically sound general theory of systemic transformation can be formulated. We are at the stage of figuring out relevant questions and identifying major stumbling blocks. Having accomplished that this author hopes to have done a useful job in compiling this volume which might be of help to other countries' economists and policymakers in their not repeating Central European errors. For economic theorists in East and West the peculiar experience of this region may well remain a lavish source for inspiration and interpretation for quite some time to come.

Notes

1. Actually, trade with the West showed a nearly 1 billion US$ surplus, with a current account surplus of 300 million in 1990.
2. For a good summary of the relevant (conventional) arguments cf. e.g. (Linder, 1990) and (Nuti, 1991).
3. Some international consultants to Hungary e.g. have repeatedly proposed more radical market-type regimes in the social security and public utility spheres than practiced in most OECD countries.

Part II
Systemic change and stabilization: goals and substance

2 Principles of privatization [1]

by Anders Aslund

In 1989 and 1990, privatization all of a sudden turned into a key issue in the formerly socialist countries. The discussion has been somewhat confused, because the intellectual preparations had been minimal, and privatization is a very complex issue, involving law, politics, justice, morals and economics. No comparable privatization has ever taken place. While the public call for 'a normal society' and 'no more experiments', there are no directly applicable precedents at hand.

In the West and the Third World, a mass movement of privatization has arisen in the 1980s, but most of the literature has been published since 1988. In dozens of countries in the world, more or less parallel developments and experiences emerge. Their preconditions, however, are very different from those of formerly socialist countries. First, in scale - while the Western privatizations have involved tens of enterprises over several years, in Southeast and Central Europe each country needs to privatize thousands of state enterprises. Second, the privatizations in the West, and essentially also in developing countries, have occurred in market economies, with a multitude of markets, market prices, dominant private ownership, a reasonably market conform legal system, and basically a market oriented thinking. As we shall see, these differences are of vital importance.

The purpose of this paper is to uncover basic principles for a strategy of privatization in formerly socialist countries and to evaluate their implications for the practical process of privatization. These ideas will be illustrated with examples. Primarily, we shall draw on the Polish debate that appears to have been the most diverse and sophisticated to date.[2] The intention is not to give an overview of how far privatization has proceeded.[3] Our focus lies on qualitative aspects of privatization. Technical issues will only be brought up as far as they may determine the choice of principles. Ownership is an intrinsically ideological issue, and sooner or later an ideological choice must be made. Still, the economist can suggest what choices are internally consistent.[4]

In order to suggest how a privatization might take place, we need to establish why privatization is required and what problems it is supposed to solve. We shall discuss general arguments, proceeding to specific features of formerly socialist countries. A key consideration is the speed of privatization. After having clarified the purpose of privatization, we shall propose general principles of privatization and discuss the problems with large enterprises in more detail.

Why Privatize?

The calls for privatization have arisen because of the collapse of belief in market socialism as a viable economic system. János Kornai (1986), and Wlodzimierz Brus and Kazimierz Laski (1989) clarify why market socialism is perceived as a failure. Yugoslavia and Hungary represent two different attempts at market socialism, but neither has produced encouraging results. Economic growth declined; little innovation took place; structural changes were minimal; quality of output deteriorated; imbalances, especially inflation and foreign debts, grew steadily worse. Brus and Laski (1990, p. 147) note market socialism has moved in the direction of an ever closer imitation of an ordinary market economy, and if this is the highest form of market socialism, they conclude: 'why insist on state ownership at all?'

A casual observation is that no successful market economy has a public sector that accounts for more than one third of employment (Sweden), and currently the public sector is perceived as in crisis in most Western countries, suggesting that it might be too large. Notably, Japan has a public employment of 6.5 per cent. By and large, Ludwig von Mises (1920, pp. 80-81) seems to have been proved right: 'Socialism is the abolition of rational economy...Exchange relations between production-goods can only be established on the basis of private ownership of the means of production.'

Today, privatization is seen as the solution to a large number of problems, First, it helps creating a boundary between economics and politics. An enterprise director should be judged by his economic performance and not by political criteria or connections. To make the enterprises independent of the politicians does not solve the complicated relationship between principal (owner) and agent (director), but it is a necessary condition for an improvement. Also in the West, state ownership is a source of corruption (customary examples are Italy or Greece).

Second, an enterprise must be economically independent in order to be exposed to financial discipline, that is a hard budget constraint according to János Kornai's (1980) terminology. As long as the state can be forced to pay additional funds to an enterprise, large work forces with political clout are likely to exert their influence. This problem exists also in the West, but it is less pronounced. True independence of state enterprises is possible, but only if they are forced to imitate private firms. Therefore, predominantly private ownership is necessary for the independence of public firms as well.

Third, only enterprises that are independent of each other are likely to compete. It is sometimes argued that cartels have done well in countries such as Germany and Japan, but the companies were exposed to intensive competition from abroad, and the purportedly good performances were far from excellent. In both countries, the dissolution of the cartels after the Second World War and, later on, the opening to foreign competition reinforced the competitive edge (Kosai, 1986), (Erhard, 1957) and (North, 1981). Demonopolization, however, must be undertaken by the state before privatization. Enterprises are rarely interested in confronting 'unnecessary' competition.

Fourth, private ownership is necessary for the creative destruction, entrepreneurship and innovation that Joseph Schumpeter cherished. In neither practice nor theory, can these properties develop under predominant state ownership (Pelikan, 1990; Grosfeld, 1990). A considerable restructuring is needed. The socialist economies have managed to transfer people from land to town and from agriculture to industry, but not to bring about structural changes within the urban sector. In the USA, 11 per cent of manufacturing jobs are lost each year (and replaced) to compare with just 0.5 per cent in the USSR (Murrell, 1990, p. 7).

Fifth, no socialist economy has ever had any rational criteria for the allocation of capital. If there are no such criteria, rational decisions cannot be made. The investment process has been a permanent black hole in these countries, which in the end turn out to have completely obsolete fixed assets is spite of high rates of investment. A sensible investment process requires both entrepreneurship and a reasonably well functioning capital market, which in turn presupposes wide ranging private ownership.

Sixth, an old but ever more widely accepted tenet is that pluralist ownership is a precondition of political democracy (Hayek, 1986). It is not an accident that all countries with predominantly state ownership have been dictatorships. Few employers accept public criticism from their employees. In a great many democracies, civil servants are not assumed to perform independent political functions or ever speak their own mind. This is an argument both for a minimal state sector and for a diversity of private owners. A worrying question is for how long the current anomaly with state ownership and democracy may last in East and Central Europe. The experiences of Latin American countries with their largely state owned industries suggest and imminent danger of populist authoritarian dictatorship with chronic economic imbalances, if privatization does not proceed fast enough.

19

Specific reasons for privatization in Southeast and Central Europe

In addition to these general reasons for privatization, there are particular reasons for privatization pertaining to the current macroeconomic situation in Southeast and Central Europe - the requirement of a *critical mass* of private enterprises; the peculiar *role of the state* during the transition to a market economy; and the *financial situation*.

A fundamental fact is that the sector of competitive independent firms must be pretty large in order to facilitate a reasonably well functioning market. Initially, this critical mass must be especially large because of lingering state restrictions, severe structural distortions and insufficient infrastructure. In the past, the sizeable private sector in Poland was a morass of corruption and economic crime, as the market was unstable (Aslund 1984 and 1985). Possibly, a breakthrough has occurred in Poland, where more than one third of the labour force is now occupied in the private sector (Rostowski, 1990). In any case, a substantial critical mass is required before the threshold to a sound market economy is passed. To judge by existing examples, this implies more than two thirds of employment, even if the marketization is supported by a liberal foreign trade policy. In addition, corrupt practices, extraordinary profits on the sellers' market and the conspicuous consumption of newly rich are bound to arouse a popular reaction against privatization, as is currently the case in Hungary and the USSR (Okolicsanyi, 1990; Aslund, 1989, pp. 167-174). The difficulty of reversal is underlined by one of Friedrich Hayek's (1986, p. 79) thoughts: 'once the free working of the market is impeded beyond a certain degree, the planner will be forced to extend his controls till they become all-comprehensive.'

Another crucial fact is that the capacity of the state is a severe bottleneck, because the old administration consisting of *nomenklatura* appointees is demoralized and distrusted. Therefore, the state is likely to manage enterprises far worse than private principals in the period of transition. Moreover, the state administration is wrongly organized and the staff inadequately trained for many of the tasks they are supposed to perform in a market economy. Characteristically, in Poland state industrial sales declined by 27 per cent, while private industrial production increased by 7.5 per cent in the first three quarters of 1990 in comparison with the same period in 1989 (*Rzeczpospolita*, 19 October 1990). Thus, it is vital to introduce a large private sector fast, because initially it alone is able to respond to new demands with flexible supply.

The role of the state during the transition is a much neglected dilemma. At the same time as its dysfunction is aggravated, it is requested to solve many strategic tasks typical of the state, notably drawing up new market conform legislation, establishing a rule of law and an impartial legal system, introducing strict monetary and fiscal policies, and initiating the creation of a modern infrastructure. The state administration appears bound to be so overstrained that health care and education are likely to deteriorate further. The state must take on some responsibility for the social costs of transition as well. As the state will be so overburdened, it is difficult to defend extensive state involvement in the management of enterprises.

Moreover, state resources are likely to dwindle because of declines in the three traditional kinds of taxes (McKinnon, 1990, p. 133). Traditionally, the remnants of enterprise profits have been confiscated at the end of the year and total profit taxes have absorbed up to 60 per cent of profits. In a nascent market economy, it would be optimistic to reap 40 per cent of the profits in tax revenues. Substantial foreign trade taxes have implied severe protectionism that has to be abandoned, if foreign competiton is to check domestic monopolies. Turnover taxes can barely remain as large, and they must be transformed - at least into standardized tax rates. Then, the previously high revenues are bound to fall. Besides, state revenues of the socialist states have not been particularly high by Nordic standards. As early as 1988, Soviet state revenues had fallen to less than 42 per cent of GNP (IMF et al, 1990, p. 10), to compare with 57 per cent in Sweden.

It would be both difficult and wrong to try to compensate for the decline in old taxes by a rash introduction of new taxes. Since a maximal stimulation of supply is desired, high income taxes appear unacceptable. Furthermore, the weakness of the legal system is a strong argument for lenient and simplified tax collection. In the transitory period, it would be advisable to apply lump sum taxes on a large scale. They guarantee certain state revenues, while stimulating supply.

Besides, the level of economic development must also be considered. In general, the Southeast and Central European countries are to be considered middle income countries, and they have not reached the level of development the high income countries in the West maintained in 1970, when public expenditure accounted for 30-35 per cent of their GNP. Also a comparison with middle income countries suggest that the current level should go down from 40-60 per cent to about 30 per cent. Since a long term disarray is to be expected in their public administration, it should be given a minimum of tasks. Therefore, the shortfall in state revenues is no tragedy, but public expenditure should be reduced accordingly.

The financial side of privatization is rather complex. Kornai (1990/a) makes it one of the main issues of privatization, drawing the conclusion that the state should sell as dearly as possible. Therefore the state should first improve the management of its enterprises and sell them over a prolonged period. An additional argument is that privatization would generate revenues occur timely, as ordinary state revenues are falling. Especially, the Shatalin group in the USSR wanted to finance stabilization with the proceeds from privatization (*Perekhod*, 1990). There is also a popular perception that the state cannot afford to give enterprises away, especially in countries with large foreign debts, such as Hungary or Poland.

The main task of privatization, however, is to create healthy enterprises with good management, which market socialism has failed to provide. Then, the most important issue is to pass through the doldrums of the transitory period *as fast as possible* in order to reach the firm shore of capitalism and stable democracy. When that has been accomplished, we should expect steady growth rates in the order of 8 per cent a year, given that the Southeast and -Central European countries are latecomers in terms of economic development with low labour costs but basically relatively skilled labour on the verge of the biggest market in the world - the European free trade area of the EC and EFTA (cf Rosenberg and Birdzell, 1986). Then, the state can soon reap greater fiscal gains, and the economic welfare will rapidly grow, as a result of economic growth. Moreover, since the common man has little money, competitive sales would probably lead to a concentration of wealth, notably in the hands of foreigners, black marketeers and the old nomenklatura, which appear most undesirable. Finally, the value of state enterprises is likely to be very low indeed to judge from the East German attempts at privatization through sales to abundantly wealthy West German companies. Although the financial aspect of privatization is complex, we should consider it secondary and fiscal needs could be covered by other means.

Gradual or swift privatization?

Our arguments amount to a strong case for fast privatization, though this is probably a minority view. A wide spectrum of economists, ranging from Kornai (1990/a) to Galbraith (1990) have argued for a gradual privatization. Kornai combines this demand with a call for a swift transition to a market economy, while Galbraith prefers a gradual approach also in that regard.

But is there a feasible gradual road to a market economy? The international interagency study on the Soviet economy notes: 'Ideally, a path of gradual reform could be laid out which would minimize economic disturbance and lead to an early harvesting of the fruits of increased economic efficiency. But we know of no such path...' (IMF et al, 1990, p. 2). As long as nobody has indicated a feasible gradual reform, we can do little but discard it as non-existent.

Galbraith (1990) maintains his old social democratic beliefs and refers essentially to Western economies. 'As to the large industrial or commercial enterprise that is the centrepiece of the modern capitalist or socialist economy, the question of ultimate ownership is no so important...in the modern mature capitalist economy, I note with emphasis, it is not about power that we should worry, it is about incompetence. What is important...is to give the enterprise authority over, and the rewards of, its own performance.' These arguments are widely disputed in the West, and they have little or no bearing on Southeast and Central Europe, where the miserable performance of state management stemming from the supremacy of politics over economics are all too obvious. If politics prevail to such an extent, there is little room for economic competence. Therefore, privatization is a precondition of a breakthrough of competent managers. Galbraith's resistance against quick privatization may be discarded as social democratic nostalgia as well as lacking insights into socialist economies and the current state of Southeast and Central Europe.[5]

Kornai's (1990/a) opposition against fast privatization is more interesting, because he favours a radical change of the system. 'I consider it desirable to increase the proportion of the private sector as fast as possible to a point where this sector accounts for the larger part of the country's Gross Domestic Product' (p. 80). However, he rejects distribution of public property on seemingly moral grounds and is greatly concerned with the financial proceeds from privatization: 'state property to be sold to a private owners should change hands at a real market price' (p. 83). Most surprisingly, Kornai believes in the ability of the state: 'But the state is alive and well. Its apparatus is obliged to handle the wealth it was entrusted with carefully until a new owner appears who can guarantee a safer and more efficient guardianship' (p. 82). In a similar vein, many are afraid of economic collapse as a result of rush privatization. Kornai wants to direct state enterprises to strong owners, forming a new middle class, making it a precondition of privatization 'that genuine private entrepreneurial motivation should gain ground and take hold' (p. 82). His general conclusion is: '...the sale of state property should not be governed by the guiding principle of speed' (p. 93).

We have already presented a different point of view. Our assessment is that state management is in a far more precarious shape; the financial proceeds are less important than macroeconomic performance; our requirement of a *critical mass* of private enterprises casts doubt on the possibility of breeding good entrepreneurs *before* privatization. Strong owners are desired, but is it realistic to believe that they will surface on a relatively distorted market?

In sum, the arguments against the highest possible speed of privatization do not appear convincing. The greatest horror seems economic collapse because of slow transition and privatization. The question is rather how fast a privatization can be pursued.

General principles

Privatization must be based on a large number of principles. Legal principles should come first. A market economy and democracy presuppose the rule of law. There is a broad agreement that property rights must firmly be assured. Such guarantees should be as strong as possible, written into the constitution and defended by an independent supreme court. Reprivatization - the restoration of former property rights - is an awkward issue. It is difficult to prove who was an owner and what a particular property right actually implies, considering new construction, improvements and damages. These questions must be solved as fast as possible, and the legal procedures should be facilitated by unequivocal and irrevocable political decisions. A natural approach is to clarify what claims are legitimate, limiting the dates or laws of nationalization that may be subject to reconsideration and setting a deadline for claims, as has been done in East Germany. For practical reasons, previous owners disconnected with the property should preferrably be offered money or bonds as restitution rather than their former assets.

The traditional reformist claim was equality between all forms of ownership. Now the debate is turning in the direction of discrimination against state enterprises (Kornai, 1990/a, p. 47). There are sound reasons for such a proposition. All equality between the state and the private sector must be illusory, as the state has so many unique levers of power. Many democracies have special civil service codes, discriminating *against* senior state employees, because of their special prerogatives. In one sense, real equality should mean discrimination against the inevitably privileged state sector. Besides, the large state sector should not be allowed to survive, and then fast transition is probably the best cure of the economy. Sun-set branches are not very dynamic.

In all discussion of privatization, we need to distinguish between at least five categories of property: typically public property, agricultural land, housing, small enterprises and large enterprises. The most difficult issue is the privatization of large enterprises, which dominates the debate. A second theme in the discussion is the privatization of small firms. In line with our reasoning, our staring point is that a minimum should be reserved as public property. Switzerland or Japan are suitable - and successful - standards.

The privatization of *land* should be comparatively easy. The economic advantages of family farms are acknowledged in most parts of the world. The obvious solution is to distribute land and fixed assets to the current farm workers. The world has experineced scores of land reforms, providing set standards. First, we must ask whether reprivatization is possible or desirable. In some countries, such as Czecho-Slovakia, cooperatives predominate in agriculture, in which the personal shares are still known, making reprivatization imperative, while in Poland most socialized land belongs to émigrés, primarily Germans. Second, should state and collective farms be disbanded or should a choice be offered? Bankruptcies might often exclude any alternative. Third, should land be distributed with or without payment? A simple answer is that if land is taken over by farm workers it should be given away, while outsiders should pay an auction price.

Contrary to our general arguments for fast privatization, there are reasons not to touch agriculture too early in Southeast and Central Europe. The countryside is overpopulated; to a large extent these countries are self-sufficient with foodstuffs; agricultural products are difficult to sell on export. Therefore, rash privatization in agriculture might primarily shake out surplus labour too early, aggravating unemployment in urban areas. In Poland, three quarters of agriculture is already private, and cooperatives in Hungary and Czechoslovakia are reasonably independent. In the USSR, though, swift land reform seems vital. The USSR spends about one fifth of its

24

hard currency revenues each year on food imports, badly needing a larger agricultural supply. A great deal of produce is wasted on the farms. Unlike their counterparts in Southeast and Central Europe, Soviet collective farms are extremely inefficient.

Urban *housing* in the formerly socialist countries is typically rented and state owned, although cooperative flats and individually owned houses are common, too. The rights of the tenants are so strong that flats are usually inherited. Rents are normally below the maintenance costs. In effect, the tenants enjoy quasi property rights that they are not permitted to transfer outside their family. It would be better to transform these rights to real property rights without any payment, as argued by the Moscow mayor Gavriil Popov (*Izvestiia*, 19 December 1990). Then, a housing market would arise instantly, facilitating a more rational allocation of housing; the maintenance of housing would improve quickly; the state would neither gain nor lose any money, because tenants with such rights would certainly not opt for paying anything for what they have long considered their due. It suffices to look at the attempts at sales of British council housing to realize how difficult it is to sell housing rented for long, and such resistance would undoubtedly be greater in Southeast and Central Europe and also in the USSR.

Most formerly socialist countries have decided on some *small scale privatization*. This seems to be the least controversial form of privatization. Small shops, kiosks, bars, restaurants and workshops can be sold off at auctions. Here, sales at auctions are natural, favouring the most efficient allocation of the small enterprises. The units to be privatized are natural business entities of an individual or a small team, suggesting direct private ownership, and no equal distribution would allow for the necessary independence of the entrepreneur. Thus, the state treasury will receive some revenue. It is important that this small scale privatization occurs as fast as possible, because all experiences show that the marketization starts on the consumer market with retail trade, services and small scale production. Typically, in Poland 161,700 new private firms - 58 per cent of the total of new private firms - were set up in retail trade during the first three quarters of 1990 (*Rzeczpospolita*, 29 October 1990).

Privatization of large enterprises

The great dispute concerns how large scale state enterprises are to be privatized. Many questions are raised. Shall the big state enterprises be sold, distributed for free or strangled to death? To whom shall they be handed over? According to what principles or prices shall they be transferred? What kind of institutions shall carry out the privatization? How fast a privatization is feasible? Each question contains several subquestions.

We shall start turning the question around, discussing what problems we want to solve at enterprise level in order to see what

25

kind of change appears sensible. A first problem is the high degree of monopolization. Demonopolization should occur before privatization and be carried out centrally, because an enterprise has no interest in breeding competitors, regardless of ownership. In addition, a liberalization of foreign trade is vital at an early stage in order to counter monopolization (Lipton and Sachs, 1990).

Second, enterprises that are technically and economically obsolete should be closed down as soon as possible. Unfortunately, both socialist and capitalist states have turned out to be almost incapable of liquidating their own enterprises. Therefore, privatization will probably be needed just in order to facilitate their liquidation through bankruptcy. Privatization would perform a necessary destructive function.

Third, many enterprises suffer from sizeable burdens of old debts, which will become excessive, as high real interest rates are introduced with marketization. The indebtedness should be done away with either discretely by the state or through bankruptcy. In the latter case, destructive privatization would be useful. A point often missed is that bankruptcy - as well as various accords on debts - are useful means of enterprise restructuring.

Fourth, virtually all socialist enterprises are wrongly composed from a market perspective, since they are oriented towards autarky. They own all kinds of subcontractors and service enterprises, even farms, which would be independent enterprises in the West and should become so under the new system. In principle, private management would be ideal for such divestment, but sometimes the task might be excessively complex and better solved through bankruptcy or a centrally decided split of enterprises.

A radical point of view is that the state sector is so inefficient and hopeless that it would be better to squeeze out the revenue that it still can generate but rather than privatize opt for the breeding of newly founded private enterprises (Murrel, 1990, p. 9). In fact, the current development in East Germany appear to point in the direction of the liquidation of 80 per cent of the employment in state industry, effectively erasing previous large state enterprises and leaving ample space for new private firms - more than 200,000 in 1990. All over Southeast and Central Europe, hundreds of thousands of new private enterprises were formed in 1990 (Jackson, 1990). It is quite possible that these new firms will soon become more important than already existing state enterprises.

There is broad agreement that large state enterprises should be transformed into joint stock companies after a certain division into somewhat smaller enterprises. The big query is how their shares should be transferred to private owners. The discussion in Southeast and Central Europe has developed along two lines. One favours fast privatization through distribution. The other argues that state enterprises should be sold through public offering approximately as in the United Kingdom or France.

At this stage, we need to introduce a principle of justice, namely to whom do the enterprises really belong. If the answer is 'to the state', it would be natural to argue for sales. If instead the reply is that the enterprises pertain to the whole population, we should advocate that this ownership is restructured so that the shares are distributed for free to the whole resident population (possibly with some discrimination by age). Finally, the idea that enterprises are owned by their workers would imply that their share should be distributed to their workers.

Another principle of justice - and political convenience - is what kind of ownership structure do we really want. Obviously, distribution is bound to provide for a more widespread ownership than sales. Objections are that no strong owners would be at hand and that ownership would be too fluid. Three groups present in the traditional socialist society that possess vast fortunes are senior members of the nomenklatura, black marketeers and non-resident foreigners. A fourth group soon to emerge consists of newly rich entrepreneurs. Neither of these groups should be unduly favoured, if a fast privatization is to be politically acceptable. It is frequently argued that if shares are distributed, ordinary people will just sell them too cheaply, so that sharks might concentrate wealth even more cheaply than if centralized sales took place, but this does not seem very plausible.

A memento is that share ownership is mostly limited to relatively small minorities. In 1989, Sweden achieved the most widespread stock ownership ever attainted in any country, when 35 per cent of the population owned shares (down to 28 per cent in 1990).[6] Next come Norway and the USA with 23 per cent in 1990 (*Aktiespararen*, no 12, 1990, p. 44). Still, many more people own shares indirectly through private pension funds.

Few keep shares for the fun of it. Widespread share ownership presupposes substantial reasons for saving. Some of the most important objects of saving are housing, children's education, health and security in general, but if there is a well functioning credit and insurance system, housing and education can be provided for loans, and insurances can ascertain health care and security. The fundamental goal of saving remains, namely old age pension. Countries with high ratios of household saving, such as Japan and newly industrialized countries in the Far East have ample reasons for saving, private pensions, children's education, health care and housing. The socialist countries, on the contrary, have had most of these services provided by the state. Then, it would be difficult to achieve a high saving ratio. If they want to have widespread ownership and high ratios of saving as Japan or Switzerland, they need to institute a private insurance system. For instance, certain percentages of the shares in all companies could be allocated to a multitude of private insurance companies that are established for pensions, unemployment and health insurance. This would breed social safeguards that the state cannot provide, a sophisticated financial structure, and pluralism in ownership.

The outstanding protagonists of free distribution of shares are the Czecho-Slovak federal minister of finance Václav Klaus and his deputy Dusan Triska (1990). Sales of shares, on the other hand, are favoured

27

by a broad Hungarian opinion, including Kornai and the Hungarian government as well as the main opposition parties. In Poland, not only the discussion but also its resolution have been more complex, involving a combination of distribution to the public, sales and discount sales to workers of the enterprises concerned.

Free distribution can be pursued in the form of shares of mutual funds or vouchers, exchangeable for shares or bonds, or distribution of shares to employees (ESOP - Employees' Stock Ownership Programmes). The last option is close to the Yugoslav system of workers' self management, that has been a forceful argument against it. In countries that have experienced a long reform process - Hungary and Poland - workers' councils were introduced in order to reinforce the independence of enterprises from the state. However, when the goal was transformed into a complete change of the system, there was no longer any need for workers' councils. They have proved particularly harmful during the transition to a market economy. In the first nine months of 1990, chief executives were dismissed at 307 of Poland's 1,700 centrally run state enterprises, and more than 90 per cent of the dismissals were initiated by employee councils, to compare with 162 during the whole of 1989 (*International Herald Tribune*, 29-30 December 1990). Still, employee ownership has remained an issue in Poland, and the Polish privatization act contains the provision that up to 20 per cent of the shares in an enterprise can be sold to its workers at half the offering price of shares (*Rzeczpospolita*, 23 July 1990).

The perception that public property belongs to the whole population, naturally leads to the idea that ownership should be reorganized and property distributed to the whole population. Free distribution of vouchers that can be exchanged for shares has been suggested by Lewandowski and Szomburg (1989) in Poland, Klaus and Triska (1990) in Czechoslovakia, Károly Attila Soós in Hungary and Larisa Piyasheva in the USSR. There are many possible variations, but the central principle is that all resident citizens above a certain age receive an equal number of vouchers, which they are entitled to exchange, within a certain time, for shares in thousands of enterprises that are to be privatized.

The advantages of free distribution are that utmost equality is achieved, massive and fast privatization is accomplished, and the preconditions for a multitude of financial markets are created. A weird, but politically important, objection is that nothing should be given for free, because then it will not be valued. However, if property is considered to belong to the whole people, this would merely amount to a reorganization of ownership. Still, the Czecho-Slovak parliament is against free distribution and insists on a certain payment (*International Herald Tribune*, 29-30 December 1990).

However, there are two specific problems with the voucher system. First, it requires an evaluation of enterprises. Even in the West, the market value of stocks shift swiftly. In Southeast and Central Europe, the ordinary market has just been born; stock exchanges are being set up; auditing is at a rudimentary stage. Then no sensible evaluation can occur. The standard idea of new marketeers is that the issue is to establish the book value of the enterprises, but that is irrelevant for the value of stocks, which is supposed to reflect the expected discounted value of future net profits. No expertise can assess that with any accuracy before most markets have emerged.

Second, ordinary people all over the world are prone to avoid risks. To them, the direct ownership of substantial amounts of shares implies excessive exposure to risk. All the more so in formerly socialist countries, where most companies may go bankrupt within a year or two. People who lose all their shares through bankruptcies are not likely to favour privatization. Therefore, a voucher scheme may raise political barriers against denationalization. Both these problems are so great that voucher schemes do not appear viable. In addition, there are technical complications. What happens if nobody wants to buy certain shares? Initial pricing might be wild. The schemes suggest a long transition period of two years, but how will enterprises function in the meantime?

The problems with evaluation may be avoided in the initial stage, if a government resorts to arbitrary distribution. In order to reduce the risk exposure, the stock holdings of new owners should either be marginal or mediated through mutual funds or possibly private holding companies. Thus, my suggestion would be that a the bulk of shares in state enterprises to be privatized are allocated to several, say 10, approximately equally large mutual funds (or holding companies), and that every grown-up resident citizen is given an equal share through a lottery in any of these funds. Then, evaluation can take place immediately after privatization. The funds are truly private, and possess the independence and means to hire the best expertise available. They should have good incentives to restructure the economy as fast and profitably as possible.

A remaining problem is how the mutual funds should be composed. They should not comprise branch monopolies. A combination could be used. For instance, each fund could receive a big steelworks, while the shares of other companies are distributed equally between the funds. The idea is that they should be allowed and tempted to start trading immediately after a distribution of shares have occurred, thus restructuring their portfolio of stocks and enterprises. After such a distribution, all capital markets can start functioning more rapidly than under any alternative scheme. The volumes are large enough to avert market distortions pretty fast. When everyone has become an owner, the purchases by others, foreigners, black marketeers and members of the former nomenklatura, are more easily accepted and less speculative. Frequently, fears of inflation are expressed but if anyone sells shares, money only exchanges hands, as long as shares are not accepted as securities for loans, and they should be too uncertain as values initially.[7]

A proposal that might appear similar, is that state ownership is transformed into state holding companies. However, there is a great danger that these companies, that are supposed to be transitory, will not be privatized. Huge state monopolies may be created. The

29

transition to individual owners must be instant, and the consecutive privatization privatized. Any decentralization of privatization within the state system is bound to breed corruption. Similarly, it would be dangerous if the state kept a controlling post in semi-privatized companies. This would probably be a source of corruption, blackmail and uncertainty.

If the political environment does not accept free distribution through some kind of mutual funds, sales through public offering approximately as in the United Kingdom or France is the only alternative (Kawalec, 1989 and 1990). Hungary has essentially chosen this option, and Poland to some extent follows the same line. Its main advantage is that it is well known and has been tried. Its outstanding drawback is that it implies a very long period of transition that will be extremely costly to society. In addition, it is likely to create a pretty unequal distribution of property, which is likely to cause populist reactions that will impede the process of privatization further. If the state ownership is not reduced fast enough, the spectre of popular discontent with privatization and resulting economic and political failure is probable.

Conclusions

Important conclusions can be drawn from this discussion. First of all, fast and massive privatization is of vital importance, as the state is even less able than before to manage enterprises. Until privatization has been accomplished, the economic crisis is likely to persist. The structural changes are likely to be enormous because of the transition to a market economy, but they are necessary and any impediment is just likely to raise the social cost of transition. The main issue is to cross the rousing river as fast as possible in order to reach the other shore and establish a firm foundation for the construction of a new market system. Hence, *speed and scale are far more important than, for instance, revenues from privatization*. In order to speed up privatization it is essential to avoid vested interests, the evaluation of enterprises, intermediary state holdings and risk exposure of individuals. The only feasible option that has emerged in the debate is distribution of shares to most citizens through some private intermediary such as mutual funds. Denationalization may be further facilitated through the exploitation of multiple channels, such as various insurance funds, which would link the privatization of enterprises with the privatization of social welfare. However, if more or less free distribution would fail for political or technical reasons, standard sales through public offerings are the alternative, necessitating a long and costly process.

Currently, Western types of sales appear to dominate the thinking on privatization in the formerly socialist countries. Hopefully, initial failures and the slow pace of denationalization will compel many to turn to faster tracks. A big bang is possible and desirable also in the field of privatization.

Notes

1. This is a further elaboration of two brief articles on these lines (Aslund, 1990 a b). Drafts of this paper have been presented at the Institute of International Economic and Political Studies (IMEPI, whose director is Oleg Bogomolov) and at Kuibyshev's Institute of Planning. Nils Gottfries, Sten Luthman and Ivan Major have read and commented upon drafts. The useful comments are gratefully acknowledged, while remaining faults are my own.

2. In Poland, a number of competing ideas emerged already in 1988 (*Propozycje*, 1989), and the adoption of a law on privatization in July 1990 was preceded by an extensive debate, offering a broad spectrum of views. In Hungary, a scheme close to a standardized Western approach won wide approval at an early stage (essentially, Kornai, 1990a). In Czechoslovakia, Václav Klaus and Dusan Triska's voucher scheme has completely dominated the debate. The Soviet debate only started in 1990, primarily with the Shatalin Program (*Perekbod*, 1990), and it is highly immature.

   One of the best Soviet discussions of privatization has been published in the governmental reform programme (*Pravitelstvennaia*, 1990). The debate in Romania and in Bulgaria appears rudimentary.

3. For recent quantitative indications, see Jackson (1990).

4. I have drawn on related papers, notably, Grosfeld (1990), Dhanji and Milanovic (1990), Vanous (1989), Nuti (1991), Jasinski (1990) and Hanson (1990).

5. Galbraith never realized what a mess the socialist economies were. As late as 1984, he made the following statement: 'That the Soviet economy has made great material progress in recent years...is evident both from the statistics...and from the general urban scene...One sees it in the appearances of solid well-being of the people on the streets, the close to murderous traffic, the incredible, exfoliation of apartment houses, and the general aspect of restaurants, theaters, and shops. ...Partly, the Russian system succeeds because, in contrast with the Western industrial economies, it makes full use of its manpower...' (*New Yorker*, 3 September 1984, pp. 54, 60-l, as quoted in Pipes 1990)

6. Typically, Sweden has a minimal household saving in spite of a high standard of living, since the state provides education, health care, much of the housing and substantial pensions and the credits system is well developed. The extensive Swedish share ownership is to a large extent a gimmick to avoid taxes.

7. Blanchard and Layard (1990) and recently Jeffrey Sachs take similar lines, though not in (Lipton and Sachs, 1990).

3 Systemic change and convertibility: a comparison of Poland, Hungary and Yugoslavia

by Iván Szegvári

Historical background

Convertibility is not a brand new objective in Central and Eastern Europe. In the economic goals of the reforming Central and East European countries - Yugoslavia (1965), Hungary (1968), Poland (1981), and the Soviet Union (1985) - the convertibility of currency was formulated as a priority objective, mainly during the radical periods of reform. These countries have also made major practical steps first towards loosening later to the removal of the monopolistic foreign trade and foreign exchange control, the decentralization and liberalization of external economic relations, and hence created some preconditions and certain elements of the convertibility of their currency. (Szegvári, 1989). However, these steps did not - and because of some intrinsic features of the system could not - constitute a consistent process leading towards real convertibility. What is more, under the given conditions the individual liberalizing steps also contributed to the general destabilization of these economies.

The sweeping political changes of 1989 and the resultant unambiguous governmental commitment to fast marketization created a new situation for convertibility as well. On the one hand, political and ideological barriers basically responsible for the built-in systemic constraints on currency convertibility have been eliminated. By the same token they implied further progress in the field of convertibility, insofar as this has become one of the basic symbols of the change in the economic system. Convertibility thus plays legitimating role for the new governments. Liberalization of other fields, of socioeconomic activity coupled with the spontaneous expansion of grey and black foreign exchange markets motivate a rapid external economic liberalization. The rapid and accelerating process of the loss of value and of confidence in the inconvertible East European currencies reinforces the trend. And account is to be taken, in this context, of the demonstrative effect of the successes of the German unification and recently of the bold Yugoslav and Polish attempts at achieving convertibility.

Naturally, it will be long and thorny path for the Central and the East European countries that will lead, mostly through an uncharted territory, to full convertibility and to a fully fledged market economy. For the tasks of transforming Central and East European economic systems no detailed instructions are provided either by the well known theoretical models of market or planned economies. In this respect, even available international evidence is of rather limited value.

What the postsocialist countries' earlier attempts at reform can provide as lessons are mostly failures. This limitation holds also for the frequently invoked West European analogies, the European Payments Union included, since actual conditions are hardly comparable.

What makes the issue of convertibility in Central and Eastern Europe truly comprehensive and unprecedented is the fact that the tasks of stabilization, liberalization, restructuring and systemic change have emerged simultaneously. It is the tasks connected with these four closely interrelated but often contradictory aspects, which are to be treated simultaneously that makes the process of transition from planned to a market economy a most exciting and most important theoretical and practical challenge.

Regarding the complex of issues of the transition to a market economy various approaches emerged in literature. One extreme is represented by the philosophy of 'quick dramatic leap into the market economy'. (Sachs, 1990). The other extreme standpoint is that of attempting a gradual evolutionary transition based on the hypothesis of a dual economy as originally proposed by Kaser (1987).

A definitely in-between stand is represented by Kornai (1990/a) who proposes a shock therapy for stabilization, whereas in terms of systemic change and its core, privatization he reckons with a long period. It is our overall attitude to systemic transformation which mostly also determines the view taken by individual authors on convertibility. The first extreme urges immediate and radical changes in this respect as well, taking convertibility as the anchor for the entire liberalization, stabilization, restructuring and systemic change. Meanwhile the incrementalist approach involves a gradual progress on the road towards convertibility, too. In his original concept, Kornai (1990/a) proposed essentially a dual track system i.e. different regulation for the external economic relations of the state and the private sector. In a recent amendment however, he, too favours a radical and uniform approach (Kornai, 1990/b).

Varieties of Actual Convertibility in Central and Eastern Europe

By the 90s four essentially different paths towards convertibility have become manifest in the Central and East European practice.

a *Full convertibility through monetary union*

Obviously, the case of the GDR is not a model to be actually followed by other states in the region, insofar as it, among others, presupposes the existence of a sister country, ready to settle a sizable part of the bill of systemic transformation. Marketization through German unification is instructive, since it provides realistic empirical estimates of the macroeconomic costs of a swift transition to the market.

b *Convertibility through shock therapy*

The textbook example of this is provided by the 1990 stabilization policies in Poland and in Yugoslavia, although the first breakthrough on this road was the 1989 economic policy turn in Vietnam (Fforde, 1990). The decisive common trait of these cases is the prime role played by convertibility in the shock treatment that had followed hyperinflation.

c *Convertibility through gradual import liberalization*

This attempt at limited convertibility has been undertaken by Hungary from 1989 on, intending to achieve full import liberalization through a 2-4-year programme. Essential components of the Hungarian convertibility version are the uniform exchange rate and the lack of a parallel foreign exchange market.[1]

d *Convertibility in the dual-track systems*

Dual track system is the cover name of fairly heterogeneous attempts at liberalization in China and the East European countries. In fact, what is at issue here is the simultaneous existence of not merely a dual but of a multiple system. Its chief distinctive mark is that in the enterprise sector two essentially different foreign trade and monetary regulations coexist: currency rationing and a liberal exchange. In its fully fledged form is appears in currency retention quotas and the institutions of a limited foreign exchange market. It is only in the latter area where foreign trade liberalization and convertibility is present. This system is operating with lots of peculiarities in the Soviet Union, Czesho-Slovakia,[2] Bulgaria and Romania. This dual régime of currency allocation used to operate in previous reform attempts of Yugoslavia, Poland and China. Duality of the exchange rate is a natural component: one is an officially fixed rate of exchange in the centralized sphere, and the other is a market clearing rate. In pathological

35

cases - as in Yugoslavia and Poland in the period of hyperinflation - the dual system may develop into a two currency system, with the foreign exchange used for internal transactions too.

In 1991 the dual system was to be developed further in the Soviet Union, although it is not yet decided whether in the limited foreign exchange market the foreign exchanges themselves, or assignments for them (Aganbegyan, 1990), or an artificial Soviet convertible currency, the 'chervonets' (Yakutin, 1990), will be in circulation.[3] In Czecho-Slovakia, on the other hand, the Hungarian option was introduced from 1 January 1991.

These four paths to convertibility primarily differ in the extent and scope of liberalization. However it cannot be claimed that they were merely different shades of the same colour. Available evidence is too scarce and inconclusive for us to solve the dilemma of radical versus gradual transition to the market order.

Comonalties and differences in currency convertibility

The Polish, Yugoslav and Hungarian versions of convertibility have their most characteristic common trait in that the national currency is only internally, i.e. for the residents convertible. In the given context, the foreign participants of joint ventures are likewise considered as residents. This sort of convertibility prevails in Poland and Yugoslavia on a declared basis, while in Hungary it operates de facto. The introduction of external convertibility and the commitment to comply with the provisions of Article VIII of IMF are seen as realistic in the near future by the Yugoslav government alone (Markovic, 1990). However, senior Yugoslav experts are skeptical about the longer run success of this operation (Bajt, 1990; Cicin-Sain, 1990). Both in Poland and Hungary, external convertibility is seen only as a long term goal. (Dabrowski, 1990; Pulai, ed. 1989).

Both of these paths to convertibility contradict in two respects to conventional wisdom, based on postwar West European experience. The most astonishing element is that both in Poland and Yugoslavia the instantaneous introduction of internal convertibility took place. While in the 50s in Western Europe currency convertibility evolved as a function of overall economic stabilization, in Yugoslavia, Poland and partly in Hungary too, it is the other way round, convertibility is the anchor for the whole stabilization. This is explained by various factors. In the foregoing mention was already made of the politico-psychological role of convertibility. Introducing convertibility governments have voluntarily submitted themselves to an objective external constraint, exceeding the conventional IMF requirements. This enabled them to enforce a strict financial and monetary policy, and provided some sort of protection against domestic pressures. *Finally, unlike in Western Europe, convertibility is a way of creating and not simply of liberalizing a market economy.*

The considerable time lag between internal and external convertibility requires explanation. Reservations concerning external convertibility stem from the fear of wild and uncontrollable exchange rate fluctuations and the concomitant loss of decisionmaking autonomy of the government. Western Europe was in a more favourable situation in several respects. The Bretton Woods system represented a stable international monetary environment. Many West European countries introduced external convertibility simultaneously, cooperating in the EPU and OEEC. The process leading to convertibility took place under the dynamic growth of their economies and mutual trade. Under the Marshall Plan it was possible to draw on external resources.[4] None of these features are available in Central Eastern Europe.

Thus small wonder that all Central and East European versions of convertibility are limited in nature. Basically, convertibility only applies to the current account items of the balance of payments and, joint ventures apart, it does not pertain to capital items. In Poland and Yugoslavia some 90 per cent of imports from the West were liberalized in 1990, while in Hungary the liberalized share was 60-65 per cent in 1990 to, and in 1991 it is raised to 90 per cent. In Yugoslavia and Hungary all the joint venture regulations are liberal. In Poland, on the other hand, strict regulations applied to both the extent of the share of foreign ownership and profit repatriation even under the 1990 shock therapy.

The controversial role of private foreign exchange accounts

As regards internal convertibility it is of decisive importance that the zloty and the dinar are formally convertible for households as well. This seems to contradict to the conventional logic of introducing convertibility, according to which the extension of convertibility to households is the last phase of development. Meanwhile in Hungary, restrictive regulation is in force limiting the official (legal) possibility to purchase an annual 50 dollars per person.[5] The background to the introduction of this scheme was that the haphazard liberalization of travel, of customs rules and of the foreign exchange controls in the autumn of 1988 led to an annual loss of 1,5 bn dollars for the Exchequer in 1988-89.

It is a common characteristic that *in all the three countries households may keep interest-bearing foreign exchange accounts in the domestic banks*. This is no new element on its own. What is new is mainly that any amount of foreign exchange can be deposited. In Poland and Yugoslavia this is provided for by the legalization of the foreign exchange market for households whereas in Hungary by the circumstance that no certification of origin is required. The motive behind the liberal arrangements has been to attract and feed into the banking system the foreign exchange households earlier kept at home or abroad. However, this has been a double-edged sword with the permanent threat of institutionalizing a two currency system. In

Hungary this danger has been aggravated by the negative real rates of interest on forint deposits. In the present day Central and Eastern Europe the spread of foreign exchange accounts appears to act as an indispensable but greatly hazardous constituent of currency convertibility. As long as stabilization proceeds successfully, it may also act as a stabilizer, in case of mismanagement, however, it triggers cumulative processes of destabilization.

With the given degree of the liberalization of external economic relations convertibility presupposes a market-type allocation of foreign exchange. In this respect the most advanced situation has been reached in Yugoslavia, where a uniform foreign exchange market is operating for enterprises and households[6] . In Poland there is a private foreign exchange market for households, while in other domains of the economy a banking level foreign exchange market functions (Dabrowski, 1990). As a real market, in Hungary just a black or grey foreign exchange market operates for households. Officially only a fairly narrow experimental interbank foreign exchange market was initiated in 1989 (Botos, 1990). For the enterprise sphere, however, asymmetric market relations prevail in all the three countries, insofar as all foreign earnings must be sold to the central bank at a fixed rate, whereas the foreign exchange necessary for imports is allocated on a semi-market basis.

As a further commonalty an officially fixed uniform rate acts as an anchor in the entire stabilization process. As a consequence of the restricted functions of the exchange rate, demand control relies on other tools of monetary and foreign trade policy. This gives rise to concerns particularly in Yugoslavia and Hungary, where the respective exchange rates are submarginal, which creates an unstable situation.

In Poland just to the contrary: the official zloty rate is obviously undervalued relative to purchasing power parity,[7] thereby strengthening the foreign trade consequences of the severe monetary policy. In 1990 a minor fall in the imports and an 4,7 bn US dollar foreign trade surplus emerged. This surplus is coupled with the 4,7 bn rouble surplus, both aggravating the inflationary pressure having driven up prices already in the second half of 1990.

Differences in the macroeconomic environment of convertibility

To begin with, there are striking differences in the three countries as regards the political backing of the governmental policies. In Poland, the victory first of Solidarity, later of Walesa ensured full legitimacy just as well as unlimited scope for action to the government. The situation has been just the reverse in Yugoslavia, where the federal government introduced a stabilization programme amidst the disintegrating political frame. Meanwhile in Hungary the conservative coalition government had by and large to carry on the economic policies inherited from its socialist predecessor.

Essential differences are to be experienced as regards the issue of inflation. In Poland and Yugoslavia inflation amounted in 1989 to an annual 244 per cent and 1225 per cent, respectively, resulting in a definite hyperinflation in the last months of the year. In Hungary inflation was 17 per cent in 1989, and with 29 per cent 1990 it remained qualitatively lower than in the other two countries (250 per cent in Poland and over 100 per cent in Yugoslavia on an annual base). Despite this, the current level of inflation in Poland and Yugoslavia is seen as an unambiguous success, while in Hungary even the much smaller figure is often interpreted as a fiasco.

No matter how paradoxical it sounds, the spectacular failure of the Polish and Yugoslav reforms of the 1980s has created a favourable starting point. On the one hand social expectations towards economic policy decreased. On the other hand, inflation has fully absorbed the monetary overhang. Thirdly, it has considerably decreased the debt service burdens and created the possibility of a large scale correction of the level of the real rate of exchange. Thus small wonder that 'deliberate elements can also be identified behind the evolution of the Polish hyperinflation'. (Kolodko, 1991).

Within the framework of the Polish and Yugoslav shock therapy, radical steps have been taken towards the reduction of the deficit. The central bank was made independent of the government, consequently a sizable chunk of the Budget deficit had to be monetized. In this respect the Hungarian economic policy has been able to take smaller steps only. The law on the (relatively) independent monetary authority is yet to be submitted to Parliament, thus in 1990 and also in 1991 the National Bank has to finance about twice as much of the governmental expenditures than its would be statute envisages. On the other hand, with issuing treasury bills and compelling the Treasury to finance part of its outlays via open market operations meaningful steps have been made in monetizing governmental debts. With the abolition of various central 'funds' of the former State Development Institution actual governmental spending in its entirety has come under democratic parliamentary control for the first time in postwar history in 1991.

Three crises of postsocialism and convertibility

Having recourse to some simplification, the transition to the market economy may be described as a continuous and simultaneous management process of three lasting macroeconomic crises, those of global *equilibrium*, of *structures*, and of the *system*. In the given approach, the process of the development of market relations and of the extension of liberalization, and hence of convertibility, is conditioned i.e. restricted or encouraged by the prevailing combination of these three crisis components.

The picture would further be complicated if socio-political factors were included. What I altogether dare to undertake is to present hypotheses on the interaction of the three crisis components with currency convertibility.

Current Polish, Yugoslav and Hungarian economic policies have focussed primarily on overcoming the disequilibria inherited from the previous régime. In the narrow sense, the Polish and the Yugoslav stabilization programmes in 1990 have proved fundamentally, and the Hungarian version mostly, efficient. The rates of inflation are relatively low. The Hungarian stabilization is overshadowed not so much by the current rate of inflation as by uninterrupted governmental overextension. The external position has definitely improved in all the three countries. The value of the current account surpluses is all the more remarkable as they were performed under fairly liberalized pricing and trade régimes (unlike in the early 80s). However, in all the three countries a considerable recession is the price of these successes. In 1990 industrial production declined by about 30 per cent in Poland, and by roughly 10 per cent in Yugoslavia and Hungary.

A direct tradeoff between stabilization and recession is unavoidable in the given Central and East European context. In the case of fully fledged market economies, too, inflation and deficits of the current account act as a mechanism for selfdefence of a rigid economic system. These become operative when distributional conflicts would require the system to outperform its potentials. (Cairncross, 1976) Shortage economies have had as their special 'mechanisms for defence' increases in intensity of shortages. The latter was managed by administrative and informal state interventions. The Polish, Yugoslav and Hungarian stabilization and liberalization programmes all aim in their core at braking these defences. The ending up in a significant recession, which is not only hard to manage politically but, if becomes a selfgenerating process, is dysfunctional from the pure economic aspect as well. The intense bargaining under the weak governments among the strong lobbies in a period of deep recession exacerbates inflationary pressures (Csaba, 1990/d). Stagflation therefore, is anything but abstract theory for these nations.

Monetary restrictions - a recipe for structural illness?

Monetary restraint has, undoubtedly had a lion's share in enforcing structural changes as well as current account surpluses and even changes in the property structure in the economic transformation and stabilization policies in Poland, Hungary and Yugoslavia alike.

However, simultaneously with the strengthening of its restrictive character and its role within overall economic policy monetary policy has become the area where structural tensions of the economy become manifest. At the same time the fact that no solution has been found to the structural crisis (which of course is by no means a monetary problem) this erodes the efficiency of monetary policy. This problem is well illustrated by the small rate of bankruptcies. Unemployment is just in its initial phase in Hungary and Poland, and it has hardly exceeded its previous levels in Yugoslavia. Structural tensions appear in two major forms: companies do not pay each other's bills, thus they are 'queuing' for their own money at their bank, whereas the dubious outstanding claims of the commercial banks continuously grows. The stock of unpaid bills in Hungary amounted to 14 billion forints and the end of 1987, to 45 billion at the end of 1988, and to 130 billion forints in the end of 1989. By the end of 1990 - including various forms of enforced commercial lending this amount is an estimated 300 billion forints. (Szép, 1990) The actual problem is partly less partly much more significant than that. On the one hand, 'queuing' is partly accounted for by mutual liabilities within a range of enterprises, and as such it is to be cleared within the monetary sphere. Moreover the 'hard core' of those nonperforming firms triggering others into arrears run mostly businesses without meeting effective demand. In the portfolio of commercial banks dubious outstanding claims on notoriously illiquid enterprises constitute a sizable chunk. In want of suitable bank reserves, the writing off of such debts would drive commercial banks to bankruptcy in a chain reaction. The maintenance of the current situation is, incidentally, serving the interest of the commercial banks themselves, since due to substandard accounting practices, even financially unrealized outstanding claims generate significant - although ultimately just fictitious - nominal profits for them.

All in all monetary policy in the quasi-market post-socialist countries functions under a crippling structural crisis, thus it becomes dysfunctional. It may induce counter-selective effects, as a considerable share of new credits is absorbed by notoriously illiquid enterprises. This is so as often they are both clients largest shareholders of the commercial banks (Várhegyi, 1990; Molnár, 1990). Monetary restrictions highly deteriorate the economic climate for the efficient state enterprises and for private entrepreneurs as well. (Kaleta, 1990; Murrell, 1990). In the given situation the burden of the monetary and financial austerity is put chiefly on to the efficient economic actors and on the households, since the losses of low-efficiency economic actors are ultimately financed by these two spheres.

The underlying structural crisis thus renders recent gains in stabilization and liberalization fragile as its fundamental constituents have not yet been addressed by the recent policies. Under the given institutional setup and property arrangements *structural rigidity will severely limit any major attempts to open up the reforming economies*, although this is what actual import liberalization and currency convertibility practically would imply.

Overcoming the structural crisis encounters major stumbling blocks. Structural tensions, caused by noncompetitive areas and activities are so pervasively in postsocialist economies that launching a general and frontal attack against them would entail a further decline of production, an increase in unemployment, further external disequilibria and hyperinflation. The underlying *structural crisis implies a protracted recession*, and newly elected governments are yet unwilling to face it.

The mostly latent crisis will be made, at least partly, explicit by the switchover to trade in convertible currencies with ex-Comecon states contributing to the global macro-level destabilization.[8]

A structural illness calls obviously for structural therapy in form of active longer term governmental target-setting over and beyond the limits inherent in restrictive monetary policies: one promoting selected areas of supply-side adjustment. This would require a resolute governmental stance vis-a-vis firms to be divested. The best solution would be if bankruptcies were initiated by the commercial banks, still the latter are themselves prisoners of the structural crisis.

Therefore the emergence of a two-tier banking system with competing commercial banks, creation of an independent monetary authority following the policy of tight money and fiscal restraint - i.e. the three fundamental components of current Polish, Hungarian and Yugoslav stabilization packages - are necessary though hardly sufficient conditions for bringing about currency convertibility. The latter would require clear governmental policies vis-a-vis bankrupt firms as well as a resolute future target setting, which would tackle the roots of a crisis which is structural in nature.

External implications of systemic change

Currency convertibility would thus require radical policy and systemic changes, which is - *in abstractu* - supported by all relevant political forces. However a fully-fledged market economy can evolve only in the course of a relatively long period. Naturally, political change may call forth lots of positive effects already in the course of transition to the market. Acquisition of property may represent a major motivation to save (including foreign exchanges). The possibilities for takeovers stimulate foreign direct investment. The spread of private businesses may considerably enhance the export potential. The structural crisis can, of course, hardly be overcome without wide ranging privatization. It is also clear that in the given specific Central European environment the systemic change presupposes on its own, a relatively rapid progress both in external liberalization and convertibility.

The major danger lays therein that *systemic change itself entails*, particularly in the short and medium run, *major destabilizing effects*, which are added to inherited disequilibria and to the structural crisis. The destabilization effects stern mainly from structural obstacles to the cardinal components of the systemic change: privatization and marketization (Kornai, 1990/a; Dietz, 1990). The fundamental issue in this respect is the continued predominance of state ownership. Unless it changes it is hardly possible to develop comprehensive market relations that are uniform for the whole of the economy (such as market clearing interest rates and prices, and marginal exchange rates). In the 1990s Polish, Yugoslav and Hungarian convertibility attempts are based on the assumption that this task is feasible to be mastered.

However, the basic assumption requires empirical verification. Some salient features of systemic change is yet to be seen. In between 1989-91 the performance of the state sector has decreased considerably. Meanwhile privatization was still in its most embryonic phase, i.e. that of conceptual preparation. Therefore behaviour of economic agents as well as of governmental organs have hardly been changed. (Soós, 1990) Despite comprehensive liberalization, selection mechanisms of the market have got going only to a rather limited extent in any of the there reforming countries. Enterprise losses can be financed through the widespread recourse to hidden subsidies: by not paying the bills, by tax evasion, by selling out of the state property, by spending depreciation on current outlays etc. Foreign investors continue to find the Central European situation too unstable for massive long term engagement. The new governments are yet to find their role in managing economic transformation skilfully, both as owners of the bulk of the capital and as guardians of the public interest. The policy of doing nothing is not the best recipe for managing structural tensions. Therefore politically motivated overambitious statements about 'having created' or 'being on the verge' of *de facto* convertibility in 1989-91, or plans to declare the zloty, the crown, the forint - or the rouble - convertible already in the first half of the 1990s deserve a good deal of skepticism. Without having first created its structural and systemic preconditions, no currency has ever managed to sustain its free convertibility to other monetary units.

Notes

1. A general interbank exchange of foreign currency is introduced from July, 1991 whereas black market transactions of the population are de facto fully liberalized since September 1989 (ed. note).

2. From 1 January 1991 Czech and Slovak companies are free to buy convertible currency for a 20 per cent surcharge to the official rate of exchange (ed. note).

3. In reality, following the presidential decree of 2 November 1990, 90 per cent of the currency intakes of Soviet firms are channeled to one central fund or another. Cf. *Népszabadság*, 4 Nov, 1990 and *Novoe Vremia*, 1990, No. 50. (ed. note).

4. The role the latter actually played under German conditions concretely, as well as the validity of the entire approach of soft-loan based adjustment financing is a controversial issue in economic literature. Cf. e.g. (Gröner, H. - Schüller, A., 1990) - editorial note.

5. This situation has - again - gradually given way to much more restrictive practices by the authorities. In December 1990 currency accounts of the citizens were formally frozen (again), whereas transfers or taking money abroad in cash have already previously, been prohibited (only travellers' cheques up to 1000 DM were allowed). Small wonder that the black market reappeared despite the exchange rate adjustment. (M.Zs. 1990) - ed. note.

6. Cf. note No 1.

7. For a detailed statistical substantiation of this point of Kolodko (1991) and Wasilewski (1990).

8. These issues are discussed in detail in the chapter of G. Oblath in this volume (editorial note).

Part III
Systemic change and stabilization:
theory and policy

4 Political economy of sequencing tactics in the transition period

by Gérard Roland

Introduction[1]

This paper addresses the issues of sequencing and speed in the transition from plan to market. The starting point of the analysis is the existence of opposed interests in society leading to potential conservative or populist opposition to the introduction of the market. Sequencing tactics is determined by the necessity for reform minded governments to take into account these political constraints. Sequencing errors can, through their adverse welfare and distributive effects, violate the political constraints faced by these governments and thus jeopardize the transition process for a more or less prolonged period. Correct sequencing tactics cannot eliminate the inevitable costs of transition from one economic system to another, but it can, through the order of adoption of economic measures, relax progressively the existing political constraints while keeping the inconsistencies of the transition period at a minimum level.

If one is ready to go further than the simple dichotomy of transition viewed as 'big bang' versus gradualism, one can show that the existence of political constraints may imply simultaneously a minimal speed requirement for the transition and a positive argument for predicting gradualist transition strategies that dynamically influence the constituencies for and against economic reform.

In the first section, we propose a framework for analyzing the dynamics of political constraints in the transition period. In the

47

second section, we will examine the consequences of our analysis in terms of sequencing tactics and propose a four phase transition scheme. In the third section, we will quickly review, in function of that scheme, the transition path already followed by the different Central and Eastern European countries.

The analysis is conducted in sufficiently general terms to provide a unified framework, applicable to all countries in transition. At the same time, country specific problems are not taken into account. We propose thus here a general sequencing framework to be adapted to specific situations.

The dynamic political constraints of transition

If a reform-minded government comes to power in a centrally planned economy, what should be done to ensure a successful transition to a market economy? This is the general angle from which we want to lead the discussion.

In that perspective, it would seem too narrow to consider that the transition period only starts with the demise of communist government. In order to understand the whole dynamic, it is prefer able to begin with the first serious attempts at market oriented economic reform, i.e. 1968 in Hungary, 1978 in China, 1987 in the USSR. This seems not only necessary from a positive point of view, it may also be useful from a normative point of view in order to help those countries that are less advanced in the transition.

Before introducing the framework, let us make a few methodological remarks. First of all individuals, not groups are the point of departure of our analysis. We want in particular to avoid functionalist and holistic arguments reasoning directly on aggregates as 'the bureaucracy' or 'the working class' as on representative individuals.

There are different reasons for taking methodological stance. One important general reason is the abundance of situations having the structure of the prisoner's dilemma. One particularly acute problem is the existence of collective action failures (Olson, 1965) which plays a role in the transition period (Roland, 1990/a). A more important reason for the present purpose is that different individuals belonging to similar social groups may have opposed individual interest. In fact, the division in society between anti and pro-market forces permeates all horizontal social classes or groups. Not all bureaucrats oppose reform. A fraction of them hopes to become successful businessmen or politicians in the new system. Similarly, worker attitudes should not be expected to be homogeneous as they are determined in first instance by individual interests and expectations.

Second, our basic framework deliberately abstracts from existing institutional setups of the decisionmaking process. Though the existing institutional framework undoubtedly influences real decisionmaking, we assume that there exist an underlying balance of power dynamics which ultimately explain the outcome of political decisionmaking. Without some underlying mechanism of that sort, one couldn't explain why the institutional framework itself may change in the course of time. This is true of any institutional change to the advantage of those in power: they can change certain rules to their advantage, but not always. They may not find a majority or they may face the threat of some pressure group or anticipate some adverse reaction they feel too weak to control. On the other hand, change may also be imposed from those formerly not in power. This is exactly what has happened in Central and Eastern Europe in 1989.

We assume a single political line of division, that between conservatives and reformers. This dividing line should be understood in a broad sense. Conservatives are those in favour of the status quo and who oppose concrete moves towards the market, whatever their ideological convictions, Stalinist or populist. On the contrary, reformers approve moves towards the introduction of market institutions. One could introduce additional dimensions, but this would unnecessarily complicate the task.

The basic assumption is that individuals determine their position on the basis of their material interest, given the information available to them. They know their social status in the existing society as well as their conditions of work and consumption, but they do not know their social status, conditions of work and consumption in the new society. However, they know their capacities, talents and preferences, as well as their age, they know the social and institutional rules of the existing system and they have an idea of the rules under a democratic market economy. This imperfect knowledge allows them to anticipate their position in the future society. The degree of accuracy of these expectations plays no role here. What counts is that individuals form expectations and make calculations on the basis of these expectations.

It is precisely because the move towards a market economy cannot be Pareto-constrained and because individuals do not reason behind a veil of ignorance that transition conflicts between coalitions of opposed interests must arise.

Certain fundamental variables allow to predict individual attitudes.

First of all, there is the gap between the perceived capacities and competence and the present social use (and future expected use) of these skills. This variable not only negatively determines work satisfaction in the existing system,[2] but also influences expectations, given the knowledge of rules of work allocation. A bureaucrat or a worker holding a job slightly above his competence, and owing this position to political ties, cannot hope to increase his position if a more competitive allocation of jobs is to be introduced. He can only expect to lose because he knows he enjoys a situation rent giving him a relative privilege over those having the same level of competence. On the other hand, a bureaucrat or a worker whose competence is only partly employed and who longs for more responsibilities will have much to win from a new system. This 'competence surplus' variable is partly independent of expectations of future income because to equal incomes an increase in job satisfaction represents

49

the satisfaction of a fundamental human need.

Expectations of income are partly correlated to the first variable and depend also crucially on the availability of situation rents. Individuals knowing their capacities can anticipate their future place in the division of labour in either system, and their evaluation of how society will determine their expectations of income. Some people may fear to have to work more than in the existing system or to receive a lower pay for the same work.

Expectations of income must be corrected by a third variable, the expectation of the conditions and level of consumption. Here also, many rents exist in the Soviet type system. The clearest example is that of the special shops and privileges of the nomenklatura. There are other more benign forms of rents creating inequality of access to consumption, and these rents represent vested interests that will be hurt by reform. Numerous inequalities are related to the place of living and to the place of work. Inequality in the intensities of shortage and in access to social infrastructure favours the citizens of big towns compared to inhabitants of small provincial towns and the rural population. The former have a disadvantage over the latter in the access to food and agricultural products. The distribution of fringe benefits varies strongly from one enterprise to another. The access to markets, legal and illegal, and to parallel activities also greatly depends on the profession or the place of living. Moreover, differences of insertion in all sorts of patronizing networks may create substantial differences in the access to consumption. Certain families have, for simple historical reasons, often got privilege of living in more spacy apartments. All sorts of advantages and privileges, great and small are thus distributed in a very unequal and heterogeneous way, along different dimensions, among the different social layers.

Whether in the sphere of work or of consumption, situation rents have two characteristics. First of all, the distribution of these rents between individuals in each social group is hardly known and difficult to measure. This is all the more true the lower one goes on the social ladder, precisely among groups one must win to the cause of reform. But individuals enjoying these rents, representing numerous small privileges compared to the norm of their social reference group[3] have absolutely no interest in revealing these personal advantages. *Informational asymmetry* is thus a key problem for any type of rent-extracting reform. In the transition from plan to market, this problem becomes ubiquitous. Secondly, being illegitimate and perceived as such, these rents can generally not be exchanged against money which means that financial compensation for their loss is highly uncertain. An individual who would be obliged for economic reasons to work more or change his workplace could thus experience an important welfare deterioration through the loss of his situation rents, even if he was proposed a higher income. The existence of situation rents strongly complicates the task of transition because it is possible that many measures that seem a *priori* socially painless, induce a heavy welfare loss for many individuals, without it being possible to detect these loses or to measure their extent. The possible constellation of interests opposed to certain transition measures is thus subject to a great amount of uncertainty and will probably be revealed only through the conflicts generated by these measures.

On the basis of our assumption, individuals will determine their strategic position towards reform by comparing their expected welfare under both economic systems. Such calculations are however fraught with numerous uncertainties. Presumably, probably only a minority of individuals will determine their strategic position once and for all on the basis of a long term calculation, either because they have great confidence in their own expectations or because their individual variables are such that there is a high likelihood that they can only win or lose from change. One would expect a great group, if not a majority of people, to have poor confidence in their own expectations and to revise the latter constantly, putting a great weight on the impact of current events and transition measures on their individual welfare level. In the transition process, it is however the opinion of the least informed that is most likely to change through time. In other words, it is precisely the behaviour of this group which will determine the evolution of the political constraints. Indeed, the attitude of the most forward looking agents is less likely to change during the transition period. Their position is, to a much greater extent, determined by a comparison of their future welfare expectations under the old system and in the steady state of a market regime. Individuals who determine their attitude purely on the basis of predetermined ideological convictions are even less likely to change their opinion but they are likely to form only a small group given the great number of changes in 'convictions' that have taken place recently in Central and Eastern Europe.

We will make two assumptions concerning the behaviour of less informed agents. First of all, we will assume them to be only one-period ahead forward looking. In other words, they take into account their expected gains or losses from the current proposed measures on the political agenda when determining, in each period, their strategic position. These expected gains or losses weigh much more than individual calculations involving a much more distant future so that we may confidently neglect the latter in our reasoning. Second, knowing that they are relatively poorly informed, they will be readily influenced by signals of balance of power when determining their strategic position, inferring that balance of power changes conceal information they do not possess and affecting their own welfare. All other things remaining equal, if uniformed agents observe a signal of balance of power change, say in favour of reform, they will tend to support reform because mimicking others can be rational when you are uninformed. Balance of power changes play here a role analogous to prices for uninformed agents on financial markets.[4]

What are the implications of these assumptions?

First, if individuals are able to assess only their individual net expected gains or losses from the measures proposed on the current government agenda, their attitude towards reform at any moment in time will depend on the cumulative relative impact of past and

51

present reform measures on their individual welfare. Indeed, as a rejection of reform implies a return to the old system and thus a reversal of already adopted reform measures, current proposed measures will lead individuals to abandon the camp of reform only if their expected loss from current measures exceeds their cumulative benefit from past reform measures, relative to a return to the status quo in the old system.

Second, positive or adverse balance of power changes have a (weak) self-enforcing property. From the point of view of normative analysis, two conclusions are readily drawn.

First of all, a correct sequencing tactics for governments consists in first implementing measures that benefit a majority and hurt a minority, and then to use this favourable balance of power change to implement measures that hurt more important interests. Conversely, wrong sequencing tactics will lead to conservative and populist backlash, delaying the transition for a more or less prolonged period. *The order in which the transition measures are applied is thus important because of the way it affects cumulative welfare at any moment in time.*

Second, speed is also important since the self-enforcing character of balance of power change allows to capitalize on favourable balance of power shifts by quickly implementing measures that hurt more important interests. The failure to take advantage of such shifts can block reform if the implicit welfare losses of the measures are important. Indeed, it is quite possible that the optimal sequencing order implies, at a certain moment of the reform process, that the cumulative *relative* effect of the transition measures becomes negative for too great a number of individuals, thereby blocking the transition. However, if the same measures are introduced at a certain speed, taking advantage of a favourable balance of power shift, the momentum of reform itself may then exert a persuasion effect, thus offsetting the negative effect of the economic measures. Not only does lack of speed make it harder to impose unpopular economic measures, but it signals political weakness, and this allows opposition to build up and strengthen itself. This might be a rationale for Lipton and Sachs's (1990) argument for speed, in the context of the Polish transition program. This is especially true in the case of stabilization where delay in decisionmaking only undermines popular support for the new democratic governments and makes the necessary measures later even more painful. Arguments for speed should however not lead to neglect the importance of political constraints. On the contrary, they must be deduced from dynamic balance of power considerations.

A third, and perhaps more controversial conclusion can also be drawn. Even though certain transition measures may temporarily hurt a majority of the population, they may perfectly well be decided in a democratic institutional framework. This may shed light on the 'paradox of democracy' in the transition period that can be stated as follows: without democracy, economic reform can't succeed either because the transition measures necessarily hurt a majority, hence no

52

majority will be found to vote them. This paradox is only apparent. Indeed, there is room for a temporary deterioration of welfare for a majority if a) previous transition measures have increased individual welfare; b) the cumulative effect of the status quo is worse than the cumulative effect of reforms; c) the mimetic effect induced by the sheer momentum of reform offsets the negative welfare effects. This result will be even more robust if we assume that individuals not only have the capacity to judge the effect of current reform measures on their individual welfare but can also evaluate the effect of the status quo in a slightly broader sense.[5]

These remarks concern successful sequencing tactics in the short term. In the long run, the gradual deterioration of the economic situation in the traditional Soviet type economy, in the absence of reform, reduces the long term welfare expectations of many individuals. There will thus tend be a slow but constant shift from conservatives to reformers, and this in itself improves the balance of power, independently of the measures taken. This means that, in the long run, reform forces are likely to become dominant, but that in the short term policy errors may temporarily reverse the balance of power dynamics.

A few positive conclusions can also be drawn.

First of all, it would be false in general to expect consistency in the measures adopted by reform-minded governments. This inconsistency of many reform packages at a given point in time is often the result of political constraints and it is not very useful to criticize it. One should however distinguish between 'bad' and 'good' inconsistency. Sometimes, the status quo is preferable to having to accept a bad compromise that will deteriorate your political position. 'Good' inconsistency however allows things to move and get unblocked. They will allow to shift the political constraints and to get measures adopted later on that are now politically impossible, they create irreversibility.[6]

Second, one should not judge the direction of the reform process on the basis of the announced long term projects at a given point in time. Politicians are generally only committed to the immediate measures they decide, especially in the transition period. These measures then induce balance of power changes that allow to bring about quite dramatic changes in the projects for the future.

The sequencing tactics of transition

This framework of sequencing tactics leads us to the formulation of a four phase sequencing: 1) democratization, 2) privatization, 3) liberalization, 4) restructuring. These are broad headings that should not be understood in a narrow sense. After briefly defining and discussing the contents of each phase from the point of view of the political economy of transition, we argue that this is also the correct sequencing order on the agenda of transition.

An appropriate discussion of sequencing tactics requires to take into account both the technical consistency aspects of sequencing as well as the internal balance of power aspects. As a satisfactory discussion of technical aspects would involve a lot of country specific issues in this study I prefer to elaborate the political aspects only being aware that it is difficult to avoid being schematic in such a discussion.

Democratization

Democratization includes not only the establishment of institutions, but also the enactment of a stable and predictable legal framework for the market economy, as well as the setting up of the necessary fiscal and monetary institutions, including an independent central bank.

The distortive political structure of the Soviet type system gave an exaggerated weight to the nomenklatura and different layers of the bureaucracy. Ordinary citizens who were not part of any of the nomenklatura's patronizing networks had virtually no say in the decisionmaking process. Moreover, it exacerbated the traditional *collective action failure* problems through the high individual cost of entering in a collective action against the system.[7] This point is important, because, even if the interest of a vast majority lie in the reformist camp, the collective action failure may still represent a significant impediment of change. The fact that the Soviet type institutional framework allows conservative interest to dominate underlying majority reformist interests is the single most important argument for advocating political prior to economic change. This is one of the main lessons from earlier economic reforms in Hungary and China and it has been voiced strongly by many authors.[8] It is also one of the few favourable lessons of perestroika.

The introduction of democracy does not suppress opposition to economic change, it simply changes the weights of various interests in the political decisionmaking process, and represents a strategic lever, allowing to unblock the veto of the bureaucracy to certain crucial economic measures that directly hurt their interests.[9]

Is it possible to introduce democracy prior to the market? There are good reasons to argue that a planned economy is not compatible with a political democracy (Wiles, 1977) or that their coexistence is unstable in the sense that either democracy eliminates the planned economy or vice versa (Roland 1989b). If this is true, one must then try to obtain the former outcome, not the latter. This implies again an argument for a minimal speed in the transition process. Indeed, as democratic mobilization cannot correct the errors inherent in economic centralization, it will inevitably lose momentum and fade away if it does not succeed soon enough in getting rid of the planning system itself.

From the political economy point of view, very few interests are hurt by the introduction of democracy. Only those bureaucrats who fear to lose power from the introduction of democracy will be directly hurt. For the overwhelming majority of the population, it represents an immense welfare improvement. As correctly emphasized by Kornai (1988) and Ellman (1989), the importance of democratic liberties for individual welfare should certainly not be underestimated in those countries. This is all the more true in the transition period where the positive contribution of democratization for most individuals allows to induce a balance of power shift that allows, at a later stage, to impose measures that hurt larger categories of the population.

The political conflicts over the institutional changes in this first phase will give clear signals of the underlying balance of power in society. Clearly, if one cannot pass a sensible law on private property, it is useless to dream of introducing the market.

Privatization

Privatization refers not only to the sale of state assets to private hands, but more generally to the introduction and extension of a private sector in the economy, as well as the increase of its overall share in the economy. Also included in this phase are the necessary demonopolization as well as other steps leading to a change in ownership structure, such as the creation of a separate agency (or competing agencies) for privatization.

Technically, Eastern European and Chinese reform experience have shown that it is possible to introduce a private sector in a planned economy. The limitations to its development are also clear. The logic of shortage tends to extend the scope of planning and rationing to the entire production (Roland, 1990a). This can however be countered in two ways. First of all, it is possible to develop private activity in sectors which do not crucially depend on rationed material inputs, either because production is vertically integrated or because the material input content of production is low. An example of the former is the agrofood chain where a heavily self sufficient private agriculture can form the base for food industry and sales. An example of the latter is provided by service activities with high labor intensity, labour being the most mobile resource in the centrally planned economy. However total independence from rationed material inputs is rare. Therefore it is relevant to enter a much more difficult way of imposing a hard budget constraint on state enterprises in order to break the hoarding component in their demand. This can not be imposed unless there exists at least an embryonic competitive capital market. Furthermore the political setup must facilitate the hard budget constraint's being credible by imposing a certain number of bankruptcies in state enterprises, that is at the core of our fourth phase, i.e. restructuring. Hard budget constraint's in state enterprises can thus not yet be credibly implemented at an early stage of transition.

Besides the limitations to the development of a private sector in a planned economy, there are inevitably distortive effects on prices. Besides their well known static drawbacks, price distortions constitute a major impediment to the sale of state assets: how to value these when prices have not yet been liberalized and have not reached their market clearing level? This problem is not always insurmountable. In some cases, the expertise of international banks and auditing firms can help a lot to estimate the value of these assets on the world market, especially if these economies are to be opened up to the world market in general and to foreign direct investment in particular.

What are the political economy problems associated with privatization? Let us first emphasize the favourable aspects to expanding the private sector. The early experience of economic reform in Hungary and China has shown that private initiative in agriculture and in the services sector can increase consumer welfare rapidly while hurting relatively few interests. However, when market mechanisms are introduced only partially, the price elasticity of supply is very low because of the indirect upstream rationing constraints. Small private enterprises which are relatively independent of these constraints might however very rapidly supply the goods and services that have always been overlooked by the huge planning machinery. This can happen under more efficient conditions than in the parallel economy. Legalizing of private activity suppresses all sorts of costs of protection from repression plus it decreases a great deal of informational costs, and it may bring a positive contribution to the state budget. The private sector brings immediately, albeit at a small scale, all the advantages of the market mechanism: rapid supply responses to shifts in demand, risk of bankruptcy related to the entrepreneurial activity, etc. The advantages are important for consumers as well as for the new entrepreneurs.[10]

The conflicts that will arise stem mostly from the greater inequalities of income arising from private initiative. Inequality of pay between the public and private sector might tempt workers of the state sector to coalize with the state administration in order to appropriate an important part of the private sector's revenue and wealth. Such a coalition would be encouraged by interests hurt by the private sector: the underground maffias and their political allies, or state enterprises losing their monopoly position. A predatory coalition against the private sector might yield benefits in the short term but would ruin its development in the long term. Such a coalition can only be opposed if envious state workers can be convinced that, as consumers, they will directly benefit from the development of the private sector. This depends partly on their access to the goods and services of this sector which in turn depends on their price. One of the reasons why cooperatives have a bad reputation in the Soviet Union is because their price levels are often prohibitive to ordinary workers.[11]

Additionally to the conflicts arising from an increased inequality of incomes, one must also count with the inequality in the distribution of wealth resulting from the privatization of state assets. Underpriced sales of state enterprises might create popular resentment, directly affecting the legitimacy of the government as well as of the new proprietors.

This inequality can be mitigated through the free distribution of shares: distribution to workers of shares of their factory, or preferrably, distribution of vouchers giving the right to a certain amount of shares. The latter scheme is fairer than the former which discriminates against people who do not work in enterprises (pensioners, civil servants making up about the half of the interested public) or who work in old enterprises doomed to close sooner or later. With free distribution of shares, one might however lose a unique opportunity of getting rid of the inherited budget deficits and of the monetary overhang.

From the political economy point of view, bold giveaway schemes, despite their appeals, are also very risky. The main argument for such schemes is speed. It allows to bypass the difficult problems of evaluation of the state assets and to denationalize them in one blow. In one such scheme (Aslund, 1990),[12] ten mutual funds receive each ten percent of the enterprises to be privatized and the citizens are allotted shares of the mutual funds through a lottery. From then on, shares of enterprises and of the mutual funds would immediately be tradable, thereby instantaneously creating a capital market as well as privatizing the economy.

Besides speed, one of the strong sides of such schemes is their appeal to principles of justice. This is however also the weakness. Indeed, given the newly widespread illusions of 'popular capitalism' and given the great incentive in such thin markets to use any informational advantage for the purpose of inside trading, cornering, abuses and frauds of all sorts, scandals are quite likely. These would ruin for a very long time any faith in the virtues of private property and entrepreneurship, giving rise to large scale populistic and right wing nihilistic resentment. A one time blur can thus have very harmful long term consequences. This is why more cautious advocates of privatization insist on the fact that the first experience of privatization *must* be a success story.[13] Kornai (1990/a) argues strongly against speed and giveaway schemes, stating that 'it is impossible to institute private property by cavalry attack' (p. 54) and stressing the necessity of the development of an entrepreneurial class. In that logic, entry and exit through the creation of private enterprises and the closing of state enterprises will contribute more to privatization than the sale or distribution of state assets.

From the point of view of efficiency as well as of macroeconomic equilibrium, (internal and external) it seems preferrable, while allowing national capital to accumulate in the newly created small and medium enterprises, to leave an important role to foreign capital in the privatization of big state enterprise (Roland, 1990/b). In order to avoid reactions of xenophoby, it is important for foreign capital to appear as agents of 'civilized capitalism' bringing in new technology and paying high wages in return for high productivity, and not to appear as 'speculators' coming to make a 'quick kill'. It is of course the role of national governments to block the way leading to situations via competent and liberal policies on the role of foreign direct investment in privatization.

Liberalization

Liberalization, i.e. the freeing of prices is the single most important step of the transition period because it introduces the price mechanism as a substitute to planning for balancing supply and demand. Exchange rate convertibility belongs to the package though it need not necessary proceed at the same time. Similarly, complete domestic price liberalization need not necessarily proceed in one blow.

One should insist that price liberalization consists not only in adjusting price relatives but also that of the price level, thus ensuring market clearing. Inflation is *not* a necessary consequence of price adjustment, it is only the case 1) if price adjustment takes place through price increases because of the downward price rigidity in modern economies and 2) if this adjustment takes place in an inflationary macroeconomic environment. In the former case, inflation should stop as soon as the price adjustment has taken place unless aggregate demand slips out of control *or* unless inflationary expectations have been revised upwards. As such events have a high likelihood and as some countries face a situation of important repressed inflation, the liberalization of prices is hardly conceivable if it is not harnessed by a stabilization programme. There is however no reason to view stabilization as a separate phase of sequencing, since, when it is necessary, it must proceed together with liberalization.

While being essential for the transition to the market, price liberalization is politically difficult to implement. In countries used to decades of nominal price stability, though coupled with shortages and long queues[14] any price increase is highly unpopular. The more the real income level must fall in order to adjust prices tot a non inflationary level, the more numerous will be the categories of population that will suffer.

It is argued that the adverse welfare effects of price liberalization are exaggerated as nominal wages and official prices give no clear idea of the real purchasing power of the population, because shortage makes many goods unavailable and shortages are suppressed by higher prices. Lipton and Sachs (1990) for example argue that price liberalization increases welfare by eliminating queues. Their reasoning is however based on a representative individual. If aggregate supply is fixed and welfare is equal to aggregate supply minus queuing time, the introduction of market clearing prices maximizes welfare by suppressing queues. Macroeconomic reasoning based on a representative individual is, however of little help in analyzing distributional effects of liberalization and stabilization.

Provided general macroeconomic equilibrium is sought for the rough price adjustment, it is possible to differentiate the adverse effect of price liberalization on the purchasing power of different categories of the population. This is possible through different instruments. Under Polish price liberalization, those who suffer less are those categories with savings and cash holdings. Even though these are nearly completely eroded through hyperinflation, spending over their current income is an option, which allows them to smoothen their intertemporal consumption level, whereas those households without savings face a strong decrease in real consumption. For political reasons, it may be preferrable to protect lower income categories through compensatory transfers. This might be impossible for budgetary and macroeconomic reasons. As a milder version of these policies is the indirect allocation of basic necessities to the most needy, or alternatively, the complete rationing of basic staples, possibly with exchangeable or tradable rationing cards. A more egalitarian policy than may, indeed prove effective in curbing inflation is a currency reform, like the Collor plan in Brazil. A currency reform can freeze savings or even cash holdings exceeding a certain amount, protecting lower incomes and hurting higher incomes. Clearly implemented currency reform can prove very effective in a hyperinflationary situation. In the latter case it is not only the monetary overhang, which matters but also the high and increasing velocity of circulation caused by the general flight from money (Cagan, 1956).

The more potentially painful the effects of price liberalization the more important it is to design those accompanying policy measures that take the existing political constraints into account.

Restructuring

Restructuring refers to the closing of non profitable enterprises as well as a shift to a new structure of production of goods and services reflecting an open market economy.

The price mechanism cannot function correctly, i.e. provide the correct allocative decisions and microeconomic behaviour if the soft budget constraint of state enterprises is allowed to persist. Hardening of the budget constraint is necessary in order to make enterprises cost conscious and responsive to demand. This is impossible unless the threat of bankruptcy becomes credible. Bankruptcies are also necessary in order to ameliorate shortages within industry by rapidly cutting demand in loss making enterprises and, more generally, by discouraging the hoarding motive in demand that creates a crowding out effect on the private sector. Moreover, the massive sectoral restructuring implies equally massive bankruptcies of non profitable enterprises and sectors.

In our view, the introduction of bankruptcy and the ensuing restructuring entails probably the most important economic conflicts of the transition period. Unemployment will appear in a labour market where chronic labor shortage was the rule.

However major structural redeployment is inevitable, implying important intersectoral movement of labor. This will probably be the main cause of worker opposition. In the shortage economy, the guarantee of employment in the enterprise serves as a basic social security device. Moreover, as demonstrated in section 1, rent-extraction is a vital issue in the transition conflicts. In a centrally planned economy, situation rents are generally concentrated on the workplace. The chronic labor shortage forces enterprise managers to offer all sorts of advantages to hoard labour. These advantages take the form of rents tied specifically to the enterprise. It is precisely those rentseeking workers who fear to lose in the first place if they are forced to change jobs, even if they suffer no loss in nominal wage. Forced labour mobility can affect all conditions of living: housing, transport, social infrastructure, availability of consumption goods, etc. The less the economy is monetized, the less equal the purchasing power of a unit of currency is and the more important are the distribution of non exchangeable rents on the basis of patronizing networks. Workers who consider that the rents they enjoy give them conditions of living superior to the 'norm' of their social reference group will tend to expect a deterioration of their own condition and will try to win the support of workers whose conditions are nearer to the norm but who are nevertheless very uncertain of their future conditions. Even if sustained mass unemployment is not to be expected, the short term redeployment of the labor force may create a high level of frictional unemployment. Workers with a very short time horizon will only notice the loss of their job and pay no attention to future prospects. They will thus easily be persuaded by more conservative forces of the danger of mass unemployment.

Closing down of big loss making enterprises, compared to the smaller ones, will be very difficult for three reasons. First, workers in those enterprises had generally a higher level of rents because managers had an easier access to the supply system, as their enterprise 'weighed' more in the administrative decisionmaking process. Second, big enterprises continue to have privileged access to politicians, even in a market economy. Finally, it is always easier to organize collective action in big enterprises.

Redeployment of the labor force is made more difficult by the widespread existence of hidden rents, reinforced by shortages and the absence of reliable monetary signals in the economy at large. An equalization of the conditions of access to consumption is required in order to facilitate labour mobility, but on the other hand, this equalization requires substantial labour relocation. The situation is thus hard to unblock. The trickiness of the task is reinforced by the fact that the hidden character of these rents does not allow easy predictions on worker opposition, which is less the case with price liberalization where informational asymmetry is less acute. Political precaution is therefore a vital ingredient. Imposing automatic bankruptcy rules immediately after price reform would create unnecessary unemployment and be politically very dangerous. It is therefore probably preferrable to start with a phase of selective bankruptcies, i.e. bankruptcies imposed from above in the case of enterprises where most indicators show and predict economic failure. These first bankruptcies will provide a testbench for the conflicts arising from overall labour redeployment. They will show how conservative coalitions form and will also be a testbench for the capacity of government to handle the social problems arising from economic change. It is also a training ground for society to adjust to the realities of the market and set its preferences accordingly.

Sequencing tactics

Sequencing tactics requires that the phases of transition are ranked in order of decreasing popularity and increasing political difficulty. Democratization increases the welfare of a great number and hurts only very few interests. Equally, the introduction of a private sector gives to consumers goods and services that the former planning system failed to provide. On the other hand, it hurts more interests than privatization and creates political tensions around the higher inequality in the distribution of income and wealth. Both phases can, if cleverly handled, bring a reserve of legitimacy and popularity that allow to surmount the two other conflicts which are much more relevant in moving towards the market economy and also much more difficult to tackle. Liberalization hurts many groups in the population as the real purchasing power of many will have to be reduced. Restructuring is certainly the politically most difficult phase, as workers will resist the closing down of enterprises employing them.

This separation in different phases does not mean that each phase should be completed or stopped when going over to a new phase. Phase two continues when phase three and phase four have started. The four phases should not be viewed as blocks that should be put one behind the other, but on the contrary, as a timing of the start of the phases.

We should also emphasize that from the technical point of view as a rule there should not be a substantial time lag between subsequent phases of transition. The coexistence of democracy and central planning is unstable. The development perspective of a private sector is inherently limited in such an economy. Price liberalization will lead to accelerating inflation if the budget constraint of companies is not hardened and if the necessary macroeconomic deflationary policy is not credibly implemented. From a political point of view, the right moment must not be lost for imposing further (unpopular but necessary) measures. Otherwise, one loses momentum and lets the economic situation deteriorate in its 'no man's land' state, possibly inducing a reversal of changes.

Any sequencing necessarily implies economic inconsistencies during the transition between the two systems. Insofar as transition cannot proceed overnight, inconsistencies are unavoidable. These following our sequencing path are far from being overwhelming, provided minimal speed requirements are respected. One may also argue: other sequencing would introduce rather more than less inconsistencies and might even lock transition in a dead alley. First, restructuring cannot proceed on a large scale unless prices have been liberalized earlier on. Indeed, applying a rule of bankruptcy is not credible unless market clearing prices have been established, giving information concerning enterprises without future. Price

61

liberalization may not lead to the expected supply response, unless there already exists a private sector with profit maximizing entrepreneurs searching for new opportunities. Of course, the share of the private sector is necessarily limited in an economy where prices are not yet liberalized, and large scale privatization of the economy can only be achieved after price liberalization. Our argument however only implies that there should be, prior to price liberalization, a significant private sector that will surely be a main constituency for maintaining and accelerating the pace of system change. Similarly, a private sector cannot develop unless there exists a legal framework protecting private ownership.

A draft country survey of transition

The former GDR has experienced the fastest transition possible. Democracy and liberalization have been introduced with reunification and currency conversion. Private activity expands quickly and widescale privatization and restructuring has started under the auspices of Treuhandanstalt, though creating economic and social tensions.

Hungary has been rather successful in the three first phases. Democracy is rather firmly rooted compared to other countries, a significant private sector has grown in the last twenty years and more than 75 per cent of prices have been gradually liberalized. The phase of restructuring in the context of the opening up to the world economy is still ahead. One is nearly nowhere in the implementation of bankruptcy rule.

Poland has since August 1989 made giant steps towards democracy and liberalization. Liberalization was however introduced in an economy where the private sector was still too small and the January 1990 stabilization program has led to adverse supply reactions in the state sector. The harshness of this program has led to a political crisis undermining the political unity and legitimacy of the new governing elite. The loss in legitimacy and public confidence will make it rather more than less difficult to go fast in tackling restructuring and introducing bankruptcies, despite the general reform accelerating platform of the new President.

Yugoslavia has also gone rather far in the first three phases. Further progress in transition, i.e. a serious start at restructuring, is hampered by difficulties related to the first phase. Nationalist conflicts create a problem of legitimacy weakening an unstable institutional framework.

At the time of writing, Czecho-Slovakia has firmly achieved the first phase, and despite very radical plans, has only made modest moves in phases two and three. Further privatization and liberalization are however to be expected, in relatively favourable conditions, whereas restructuring will not prove less painful than in the GDR.

The Soviet Union has made tangible moves in phase one and two but steps towards liberalization are blocked at least since 1988 and reversed at the turn of 1990/91. Measures initiated since 1985 have created a huge macroeconomic disequilibrium necessitating tough stabilization measures that will make liberalization even more painful. The deteriorating economic situation has undermined Gorbachev's credibility and increased nationalist tensions, having lead irreversibly to the disintegration of the Soviet Union. Only consolidation measures related to phase one, i.e. a stabilization of the legal and institutional framework, could provide the necessary credibility and legitimacy for further moves towards privatization and liberalization.

Bulgaria and Romania are still at the very beginning of stage one, as no legitimate power is emerging. Very small progress is made in the creation of a private sector.

Conclusion

We have proposed in this chapter a framework for analyzing the effect of political constraints (in the broad sense) on the transition i.e. balance of power constraints rooted in the structure of the population. Successful tactics consists in creating a dynamic balance of power advantage by introducing measures in increasing order of their political difficulty and in decreasing order of their popularity. We have proposed on that base a four phase sequencing: democratization, privatization, liberalization and restructuring. We also quickly reviewed on the basis of that framework the evolution of the different Central and Eastern European countries.

If these four conflicts have been passed successfully, one may consider that the Rubicon has been passed and that the transition to the market economy is essentially completed. Then comes the time for the consolidation and the handling of the 'routine' problems of the market economy: inflation, unemployment, poverty, tax evasion, pollution and many others.

Notes

1. I am grateful to M. Aglietta, A. Aslund, L. Csaba, M. Dewatripont, W. Maciejewski and P. Rutland for very useful comments on previous versions of this study.
2. Work satisfaction is rarely taken into account by economists. Sociological research on Soviet work conditions shows it to be of crucial importance. For an overview, see Roland (1989a, Ch.5).
3. See Akerlof (1984) on social reference groups and the importance of this concept in the analysis of social behaviour.
4. See e.g. Grossman (1976, 1977) or Orléan (1990).
5. For a formal analysis of economic reform and dynamic political constraints, see Dewatripont and Roland (1990) who show how, in a dynamic game-theoretic framework with rational individuals, a majority can vote rationally for their welfare deterioration.
6. A good case in point was the political reform decided at the 19th conference of the Soviet Communist Party in 1988. The measures adopted (reinforcing the role of the Soviets and introducing multiple candidatures) were rather modest but shifted slowly the centre of gravity of

power from the Central Committee to the People's Congress and created an irreversible move towards political pluralism. In February 1990, Gorbachev achieved what still a few months before seemed unachievable, by winning a vote to abolish the monopoly of the Communist Party.

A case of 'bad inconsistency' is probably the 1987 economic reform in the Soviet Union where the relaxation of central controls led to increased macroeconomic imbalances, undermining perestroika and increasing, instead of decreasing, the difficulty of further transition measures, such as price liberalization.

7. This individual cost is associated with the public good character of collective action. Romanian peasants, living far from Bucharest or Temesvár benefitted from the fall of Ceausescu, while not participating in the popular uprising.

8. See for example Brus (1975) or Ferge (1990).

9. A widespread objection to the precedence of the political over the economic reform is that right wing dictatorial regimes have proved compatible with the market economy. This argument is fallacious because it overlooks the specificity of the Soviet type system where economic and political power was in the hands of the state bureaucrats whose private interests do not in most individual cases coincide with a system of private property.

10. However, these gains tend to be eroded if reforms stagnate and thus even some of the small private firms may become monopolists (ed note).

11. Among other reasons are the evident links of many cooperators with the maffia and the traditional Russian dislike of profiteering.

12. For similar schemes, see Blanchard and Layard (1990), Feige (1990).

13. Grosfeld (1990). Another argument against such 'instant privatization schemes' that we will not develop here is that these holdings or mutual funds are not genuine private firms but quasi-state privatization agencies in the best case, new state ministries in the worst case.

14. Queues *can* socially be preferred to the price mechanism as a rationing mechanism. See Roland (1990c).

5 Experiences of IMF stabilization policies in Latin America and in Eastern Europe

by Paul Dembinski and Jacques Morriset

Introduction

Although IMF stabilizing policies have been increasingly subject to criticism, the role of this institution has only gained in importance in Latin America and, recently, in Eastern Europe.[1] This move was supported by the majority of those countries in which the IMF has recently intervened, but was criticized by most industrialized countries. There are at least three explanations why countries in difficulty continue to turn to the IMF: the need of foreign exchange, of winning IMF approval in order to gain the confidence of commercial banks and of gaining popular support for domestic austerity. However, apart from these essentially political reasons, the question remains: to what extent will the IMF be able to meet the challenge of securing balanced growth for developing countries and Eastern Europe?

Our aim, in this chapter, is to draw attention to the growing inadequacy of IMF advocated measures to solve the problems of the countries concerned. The eruption of the debt crisis and recent events in Central and Eastern Europe have changed the international community's expectations concerning stabilization programs: the goal of economic growth has come to play a major role. Although the IMF seeks to take this evolution into account by modifying its stabilization programs, which are currently called 'adjustment policies', in our view it is still a prisoner of a theoretical frame of reference inherited from the 1950s and 60s, i.e. of 'the monetary approach to the balance of payments'.

The theoretical framework used by the IMF is simplified intentionally, in order to identify a certain number of economic policies with unambiguous results. For example, it is supposed that a credit contraction will simultaneously cause a fall in the inflation rate and an improvement in balance of payments performance, without affecting output levels.

The establishment of a relationship between credit and aggregate supply allows us to reach three important conclusions which challenge the grounds for IMF stabilization programs. In section 2, we present a brief evaluation of the results of IMF stabilization programs. Section 3 summarizes the monetary approach to the balance of payments seen however, from a different point of view. In section 4, we bring certain limits of this particular theoretical framework to the foreground, by showing that the relationship between financial (credit) and real variables is more complex than the one underlying the theoretical model used by the IMF. And finally, in section 5, we take a different point of view from that on which the IMF bases its stabilization programs, which assumes that the factors at the root of imbalance between aggregate supply and demand are above all business-cycle factors, in Eastern Europe as well as in Latin America.

IMF stabilization policies: a working assessment

In the last ten years much research has been done to evaluate the results of IMF stabilization programs (see Edwards, 1989 for a good summary). Most of the authors have not gone beyond comparing the evolution of the most important variables before and after the IMF's intervention in a particular country, or comparing the economic performance of countries who benefited from IMF assistance with that of those who did not. The conclusions drawn from this research can be summed up in the following way:

'On average, the programs have resulted in a positive (though not significant) effect on the balance of payments, in a significantly positive effect on the current account, in a statistically non significant reduction in inflation, and in a significant reduction in the rate of the output growth.' (Edwards, 1989)

Insofar as the IMF's statutory role consists in attacking balance of payments problems in order to protect the international monetary and financial system,[2] these achievements may, on a superficial level, appear to be satisfactory. However, when the debt crisis erupted in 1982, the limits of this objective were shown, and the necessity of taking into consideration the economic growth of the countries in difficulty became apparent. It was officially recognized by the IMF, with the advent of the Baker plan (1985), that a country cannot make durable progress in equilibrating its balance of payments unless it also achieves sufficient economic growth.[3]

Thus between 1960 and 1980 the international community's

expectations concerning the IMF's stabilization policies changed radically. Recent events Central and in Eastern Europe have underscored the importance of economic growth (see *IMF Survey*, 14. May, 1990). Even if certain Central and Eastern European countries are heavily indebted (Hungary, Poland, Yugoslavia), the success of current political and social changes depends on establishing an acceptable growth rate during the transition to a market economy. Again, the goal is not only to equilibrate the balance of payments (one could almost say that this goal is becoming one of secondary importance), but above all to provide the necessary conditions for economic growth.

Therefore, in the last three years, the IMF has stimulated a theoretical discussion about the relationships between external equilibrium and economic growth, and has added a second component to its traditional program of policies of expenditure cuts: supply-side policies designed to promote structural changes in the economy.[4] Stabilization policy consists in a short term intervention designed to balance financial flows in the economy rapidly, whereas structural policy is a medium term plan of action.

In terms of institutional innovations, a structural adjustment facility has been set up, as well as a reinforced structural adjustment facility and a compensatory financing facility. However, in spite of these measures, there is an increasing gap between the goals of IMF programs and the expectations of countries in difficulty. In the following sections, we will summarize the theoretical model used by the IMF in order to point out some of its limits.

The monetary approach to the balance of payments

The theoretical model currently used by the IMF was developed by Polak and his colleagues at the end of the 1950's. This author sought to clarify the relationships between the monetary sector and the balance of payments, in the case of a small economy.

This model is known today as the monetary approach to the balance of payments. The simplest version of the model is summarized in table 1 below - the definitions of the variables are given in the appendix (see Edwards, 1989 or Khan, 1990).

Public credit (δD_g), private credit (δD_p) and the nominal exchange rate (δe) are used to obtain a target levels of inflation (δP_d) and foreign exchange reserves (δR). This model's virtue lies in its intentional simplicity, propitious to identifying easily applied economic policies and easily interpreted results.

The model Polak suggests can clearly be seen rather as a general frame of reference than as a rigid, definitive model. Thus, our aim is not to make this model more complicated by refining it (introducing several assets, an intertemporal, dynamic framework, rendering some of the endogenous variables exogenous etc...), but to point out the limits of this analytical framework as concerns the links between the inflation rate, the GNP and external equilibrium. More precisely, our intention is to show that a credit contraction policy does not necessarily result in a current account surplus and in a decline in the inflation rate, as the monetary approach to the balance of payments predicts it will. This is an important point, because it is useful to keep in mind that the restriction of credit is the most currently used tool of the IMF in its stabilization programs in Latin America as well as in Eastern Europe.[5]

Table 1.
Structure of the model used by the IMF

targets	endogenous variables	exogenous variables	tools
δR	δY	δy	δD_p
	δM	P_f	δD_g
δP_d	δP	E_{-1}	δD_g
	Z	Z_{-1}	
	δF	δF_p	δe
	$T\text{-}D_g$	δF_g	

Source: M.S. Khan et al., (1989), p. 163.

We shall begin by summarizing the effects of a credit contraction policy as they appear in the traditional IMF model. Then we shall present the consequences of the same policy in the more sophisticated models recently developed by IMF researchers (Khan 1989 and 1990). Finally, in the following section, we shall suggest an extension of this model which takes into account the possible impact of a change in credit on aggregate supply and demand.

The traditional IMF model can be summarized by the following two equations:

(1) $y^s = y$
(2) $\delta m^s - \delta m^d = 0$

Equation (1) states that the level of real GNP (y) is assumed to be constant by the monetary approach to the balance of payments, whereas (2) describes a money market flow equilibrium. As a disequilibrium in the money market has its counterpart in the goods and services market, then equation (2) can be modified as follows:[6]

(3) $(\delta m^s - \delta m^d) = (A^d - y^s)$ with $A^d = c + i + e - z$

where A^d represents aggregate demand, c public and private consumption expenditure, i investment, e exports and z imports.

If we accept the hypothesis that the goods and services market adjusts only progressively:

(4) $\delta P = \Phi(A^d - y^s)$

where Φ represents an adjustment parameter whose value is between O and 1.

The system of equations (1)-(4) makes it possible to track the impact of a credit contraction on the output level, on the inflation rate and on the balance of payments of an economy. By adopting the hypothesis that interest rates are fixed, the authors of the IMF model assumed that monetary policy would have no effect on interest rates, in keeping with the monetarist tradition. If this hypothesis has long seemed too strong (for followers of the Keynesian approach at any rate), it is justified today by the growing recourse to credit rationing. Recently, numerous authors have shown that credit rationing exists not only in developing countries (see for example van Wijnbergen, 1983 or Fry 1988), but also in industrialized countries see for example (Blinder, 1987) or (Stiglitz, 1988).[7] This hypothesis also corresponds to contemporary reality in Central and Eastern European countries (Dembinski 1988).

In this context, the quantity of credit (δd) - and no longer the cost of credit - becomes a determining variable likely to influence the consumption and investment expenditures of economic agents. Therefore, we can formulate our consumption and investment functions respectively in the following way.[8]

$$(5) \quad c \quad = \quad c(y, \delta d) \qquad c_1 > O \qquad \text{and } c_2 > O$$
$$(6) \quad i \quad = \quad i(y, d) \qquad i_1 > O \qquad \text{and } i_2 > O$$

We assume that a change in real credit (δd) influences consumption and investment positively. We conserve the demand for money function as it is specified in the monetary approach of the balance of payments and we construct the following export (e) and import (z) functions:

$$(7) \quad \delta m^d = \quad m(y) \qquad m_1 > O$$
$$(8) \quad e \quad = \quad e$$
$$(9) \quad z \quad = \quad z(y) \qquad z_1 > O$$

In order to simplify, we assume that exports are exogenous and that only the level of income exercises an influence on imports. By substituting equations (5), (6), (7) and (9) into the budget constraint of the economy (A_1), the following constraints appear:

$$(10a) \quad 1 \quad = \quad c_1 + i_1 - z_1 + m_1$$
$$(10b) \quad 1 \quad = \quad c_2 + i_2$$

By substituting equations (5), (6) and (9) into (4), we can reformulate the latter in the following way:

$$(4') \quad \delta P \quad = \quad (a(y, \delta d) - y) \qquad \text{with } a_1 = 1 - m_1 \text{ and } a_2 = 1$$

In order to track the repercussions of a change in credit on the inflation rate (δP), we differentiate equation ($4'$) with reference to credit. However, since the economic policy tool here is the nominal interest rate (δD) and not the real interest rate (δd), the following transformation must also be carried out:

$$(4'') \quad \delta P \quad = \quad (a(y, \delta D - P) - y)) \qquad \text{with } d = \delta D - \delta P \text{ if } P = D = 1$$

Hence, the effect of a change in the nominal credit rate ($d\delta D$) can

69

be deduced:

(11) $d\delta P/d\delta D = \Phi/(1 + \Phi) > O$

We can see that a credit contraction results in a decline in the inflation rate and that the less rigid the price level, the greater this decline will be.

The influence of a decline in credit on the output level is nil $(dy/d\delta D = O)$ since the latter is exogenous by hypothesis, while its impact on the balance of payments is positive:

(12) $d\delta R/d\delta D = (\Phi/(1+\Phi) - 1) < O$

These are the results usually predicted by the monetary approach to the balance of payments.

'A credit contraction thus results in reduced domestic inflation and improved balance of payments performance.' (Khan et al. /1990, p. 161/).

Polak's approach is presented graphically in figure (1). Equation (1) is represented by the YY line, and equation (4) by the PP line. A credit contraction results in a decline in consumption and investment expenditures, which is expressed by a downward shift of PP. Excess supply created thereby results in a reduced inflation rate and an improvement of the current account and the balance of payments performance.

This brief review of the effects of a credit contraction as they are established in Polak's model permits us to draw attention to the limits of this approach. In particular, we can see that this model is unable to explain a medium term slowdown in economic growth which has been one of the main results of IMF stabilization programs in recent years.

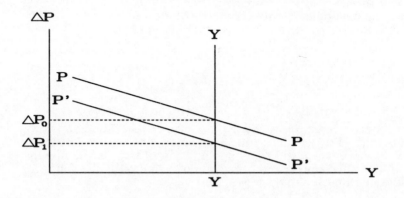

Figure 1   The traditional IMF model

70

Recently several IMF researchers have become aware of the inadequacies of their theoretical tool and in order to remove them have sought to integrate credit reduction impact on the output level into their frame of reference. Therefore, they have introduced a simple growth model into the monetary approach to the balance of payments (Khan et al., 1989, and 1990). This extension can be shown by changing the aggregate supply function in thef following way:[9]

$$(1') \quad y^s = y(\delta P) \qquad\qquad y_1 > O$$

The output level is not constant here, but varies positively with the inflation rate.[10] Graphically, the YY curve now has a rising slope.

As in figure 1, a credit contraction is expressed by a downward shift of PP. However, the impact of the inflation rate will not be as strong as before because the excess supply will be partly reduced by the decline in the output level.[11] The authors of this model come to the conclusion that 'overall the results are consistent with the standard view that a reduction (expansion) in domestic credit will reduce (raise) prices, diminish (increase) output, and improve (worsen) the balance of payments' (Khan and Montiel 1989, p. 294)).

A key element missing in the IMF model: the role of credit

The results presented above were obtained under the assumption that a change in credit would have no direct influence on aggregate supply. This hypothesis seems misguided since companies resort to bank credit to finance their business activities in the majority of developing countries. In fact there is practically no substitute for credit in these countries because a stock market is virtually nonexistent. This explains why it is the banks who generally meet major financing needs in terms of current credit (van Wijnbergen 1983), stocks (Blinder 1987) and finally investments.[12] In these

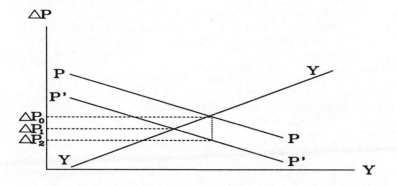

Figure 2 The new IMF model

circumstances, it is likely that a significant, positive link exists between credit and aggregate supply.

We introduce this relationship into our presentation by considering equation (1') to be the producers' target supply function. That is:

$$(1') \quad y \;=\; y\,(\delta P)$$

We assume that this target output level (y^*) can only be attained gradually, and that this adjustment mechanism is linear:

$$(13) \quad y^s \;=\; \beta(y^* - y_{-1}) \qquad \text{with } 0 < \beta < 1$$

where β represents the speed of adjustment from target to current output. It is influenced by the amount of credit made available to companies:

$$(14) \quad \beta \;=\; b(\delta D) \qquad\qquad b_1 > 0$$

It is reasonable to assume that the more bank credit is available, the more easily companies will be able to attain target output. By substituting (1') and (14) into (12) we obtain the following actual aggregate supply function:

$$(15) \quad y^s \;=\; h(\delta P, \delta D, y_{-1}) \qquad h_1 > 0, h_2 > 0 \text{ and } h_3 < 0$$

Equation (15) is compatible with the profit-maximization hypothesis for companies. First the target output level is determined as a function of the inflation rate, and subsequently the variables likely to influence are determined.

Armed with this new aggregate supply function, it becomes instructive to study the consequences of a credit contraction. Graphically, all other factors remaining constant, a credit contraction results not only in a downward shift of PP, but also in an upward shift of YY, i.e. in a slowdown in the speed of adjustment, reducing the output level.

Under these conditions, the effects of a credit contraction on domestic inflation and on the balance of payments are ambiguous, since it simultaneously affects aggregate supply and demand. This result contrasts with those obtained in the preceding models. If aggregate supply is affected more than is aggregate demand, the contraction policy results in increased domestic inflation and a worsening of the balance of payments. This case not only may occur, but often has in developing countries, when consumer credit is marginal and companies are highly dependent on bank credit.

Generally speaking, when comparing the results of this model with those of the IMF, it becomes clear that the latter have undoubtedly (i) underestimated the effect of a credit contraction on output; (ii) overestimated its effect on inflation and; (iii) overestimated its effect on the balance of payments performance. These results are important since not only do they challenge the theoretical framework used by the IMF but also the basis of the stabilization programs currently advocated by this institution.

A second limit in the IMF's analytical framework has became

apparent with changes in overall priorities after the debt crisis (see section 2). In fact, the IMF analytical framework fails to take into account the interdependence between short term targets - external equilibrium and inflation - and medium term ones - economic growth.[13] We have seen that if output level is not exogenous, inflation growth and foreign exchange equilibrium targets become inextricably linked. In particular, credit contraction may influence output level in a very unfavourable manner. This effect worsens in the medium and long term and can turn the initial measures on domestic inflation and external equilibrium backfire.[14] Paradoxically, stabilization policy is only an attempt by the state to catch up on itself, while its justification can really be seen only in the medium term: by the quality of the 'second wave' effects it sets in motion.

A third limit of the IMF's theoretical approach is becoming apparent in the light of the failure of Yugoslavia's stabilization program and the mixed results of the Polish program in 1990. Systemic characteristics of these countries make exclusive recourse to schemes derived from market economies risky.

Taken together, the limits identified in this section change the nature of the debate surrounding IMF stabilization policies. The question at hand is no longer how to continue refining the monetary approach to the balance of payments, but rather to figure out whether or not this way of dealing with quasi-market and developing economies positively hinders the IMF in correctly evaluating the specific measures which each country should adopt to adjust its economy.

The gap between the IMF's prescriptions and the needs of Latin America and Eastern Europe: a diagnostic problem

The economic indicators generally used (growth rate, inflation

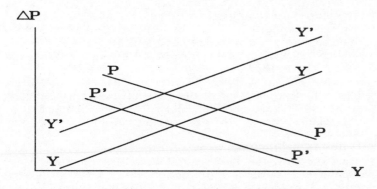

Figure 3 The complete model

73

rate, monetary and balance of payments aggregates) merely describe established facts. Their interpretation, in keeping with the approaches of Keynes and the monetarists, takes into account business cycle fluctuations above all, and scarcely recognizes the existence of structural aspects, totally ignoring systemic and institutional ones. Indeed, if aggregate supply and demand imbalances were due only to business cycle fluctuations, a credit contraction policy would be justified. However, when the causes of imbalances are structural or systemic this approach attacks only the symptoms and not the root of the problem.

The classification of potential causes of disequilibrium between aggregate supply and demand into three categories should not mislead us by its apparent simplicity. In fact, causes of imbalances are complex and differ from country to country. Enlarging the theoretical range of possible factors to include systemic and structural causes leads us naturally to seriously question the IMF practice of having recourse only to business cycle oriented policies, under any circumstances. Tackling the difficulties inherent in seeking the right diagnostics is a different approach, contrasting with the uniformity of IMF stabilization policies. The latter are applied to developing countries with differing characteristics and, recently, to countries seeking to change their economic systems. The idea that the causes of imbalances are not merely business cycle fluctuations leads us to challenge the sequencing of IMF supported policies and to prescribe first drawing up structural or systemic policies and subsequently stabilizing the economy, rather than the other way around. This reversion of IMF practices is fundamental. The idea may be illustrated by Franco's (1990) argument challenging the idea that stabilization in several Central European countries after World War I was achieved thanks to the reduction in the budget deficit. Franco's explanation is that the reduction of the budget deficit was not the cause of the fall in the inflation rate but rather a consequence of that fall. 'True tax reform had taken place at some point before the stabilizations...All these programmes were specifically designed to address the fiscal issue, but the fact that they failed in their purposes, it suggests instead that fiscal balance was not a sufficient condition for stabilization at a moment when other fundamental causes of inflation were still in full work' (Franco, 1990, p. 184).

In sum, inflation was above all due to structural problems resulting from the disintegration of the Austro-Hungarian Monarchy and the resolution of those problems allowed the state budget to be put back into balance, through the disappearance of the Olivera-Tanzi effect.

This sheds new light on the reasons for the failures of Argentina's IMF supported program, the 1985 Austral plan. This effort neglected the interdependency between short and medium term goals (see section 3) and did not deal at all with the inefficiency in the financial sector. Of course, certain observers may consider the poor functioning of Argentina's financial intermediaries as a consequence of high inflation and, in accordance with the IMF point of view, of a large budget deficit. Still, in our opinion it is rather a cause than an outcome consequently a reform of Argentina's financial system should precede all other attempts to stabilize this economy.

The IMF supported that the Polish government launched in the beginning of 1990 was based on credit contraction accompanied by a drastic reinforcement of budgetary discipline, an attempt to control wage levels and on introducing currency convertibility. This application of the monetary approach to the balance of payments in Poland does not take into account the fact that credit does not play the same role there as in a market economy, for essentially systemic reasons. Enterprises were not operating with a hard budget constraint, the role of the monobank was its furnishing the financial needs of detailed governmental targets set in physical form, the interest rate has never performed the role of allocating financial resources, and the state budget has since the mid 80s, automatically contributed to money creation. The outcome of a credit contraction in such a system is unpredictable. As long as Polish companies are not full-fledged economic agents, hopes placed in restrictive monetary policies are illusory. This is all the more so when the banking system continues to be shaped by its recent bureaucratic monobank past. (Dembinski, 1988). What is more, even if Polish companies were to be privatized and the systemic obstacles described above were to gradually disappear, aggregate supply and demand imbalances would not have the same character in Poland as in a market economy. A major problem in centrally planned economies has always been the production of goods for which no effective demand exists. Thus, imbalances between aggregate supply and demand is constituted of a series of disequilibria in individual markets, of which certain are in the state of excess supply and others of excess demand. There is no direct parallel to this situation in a market economy. In such a context, the consequences of a standard adjustment program would be doubly negative for the output level. On the one hand, companies producing in excess supply conditions would tend to disappear (Rostowski 1989). On the other hand, factor relocation to be fostered by the transition of a centrally planned economy to a market economy could be hindered both by inherited institutional inadequacies of capital flow and by the very policy of credit contraction. In the light of the preceding analysis, wouldn't it be prefer able first to adopt the indispensable systemic and structural reforms, and only afterwards undertake stabilization in postcommunist economies with the instruments used in market economies?

Conclusion

In this chapter we have sought to understand why the IMF stabilization policies do not always suit to the needs of the countries for which they were designed. Taking the theoretical framework used by the IMF as a starting point, and the evolution of the goals of the adjustment policies, three explanatory factors have been identified.

First of all, we have shown that the monetary approach to the balance of payments is based on a controversial hypothesis concerning credit. As a result, the hypothesis about credit influences the effects of a restrictive policy on growth, inflation and the balance of payments.

Secondly, the theoretical framework of the IMF does not sufficiently take into account the interdependency between growth and stabilization targets, whereas in reality they are inextricably linked.

Thirdly, even if a stabilization policy were able to tackle the business-cycle sources of macroeconomic imbalances, it does not take the structural and systemic aspects of adjustment into consideration.

While a theoretical framework exists for fine-tuning of business-cycle fluctuations, it is more difficult to generalize about problems which are structural, and especially systemic, in nature. The human and financial resources required to become familiar with the structural and systemic characteristics of each country, and to elaborate appropriate measures, are far greater than could conceivably be provided by the IMF. Therefore, the role of the IMF could change, and evolve, above all seeing to it that the business-cycle policies it advocates are coherent with - or rather, take place in the context of - a more comprehensive program of structural and systemic measures elaborated by the authorities of the country concerned.

Appendix to Chapter 6

In general the real variables are symbolized by small letters, and the nominal variables by capital letters.

δP	= change in foreign exchange reserves
δP_d	= change in domestic price level
δY	= change in nominal GNP
δM	= change in money supply
δP	= change in price level
Z	= imports
δF	= foreign asset flows
$T - C_g$	= state budget
δy	= change in real GNP
P_f	= foreign price level
δF_p	= private foreign asset flows
δF_g	= public foreign asset flows
δD_p	= change in private credit (nominal)
δD_g	= change in public credit (nominal)
δe	= change in nominal exchange rate
E	= exports
δP	= inflation rate
δd	= change in real credit
y	= GNP level
δm^d	= flow demand for nominal money balances
δm^s	= flow supply of money

Ad   = aggregate demand = c + i + e -z
i   = total investment
c   = total consumption expenditure

Notes

1. A preliminary version of this paper have been presented in French at the 7éme Journées d'Econome Monétaire et Bancaire (June 1990 in Caen) present version has been established with the help of Mrs. Barbara Schlaffer, and thanks to the research grant No. 4028 - 29272 of the Swiss National Research Fund.

2. See article 1 of the IMF statutes which states that this organization must help member countries correct their balance of payments disequilibria.

3. The fact that the international community, including the IMF, underestimated the importance of the relationship between growth and external equilibrium in the 60s and 70s can largely be explained by the fact that until the mid 70s satisfactory economic growth took place in the majority of developing countries. In this context, the ensuing costs - in particular social costs - of these adjustment programs were rarely unacceptable. True, IMF interventions were less numerous and of a more limited character than during the 80s.

4. For a more detailed description, see for example IMF, (1989) or Guitan, (1987).

5. According to Edwards (1989, p.33) the control of monetary aggregates and credits was required in 97 per cent of the IMF stabilization programs over the period 1983-85 (the control of credit intended for the public sector was expected in each and every case).

6. Given that in a model with two goods (goods plus services and money) the budget constraint can be expressed as:

    (A1) $y + f + d = c + i + m^d$

    with (A2) $d = m^s - R$

    (A3) $R = e - z + f$

    By substituting, successively, (A2) and (A3), we obtain equation (3).

7. Nevertheless, we might point out that credit rationing in developing countries is often carried out by the manipulation of interest rates, whereas in industrialized countries its explanation is based on modern information theories.

8. For a formal proof, see (Morisset, 1989) or (Blejer and Khan, 1984).

9. Notice that this supply function is inconsistent with the rational expectations hypothesis which states that an expected reduction of the inflation rate will not have any effect on the output level.

10. In Khan and Montiel's model, the positive link between the inflation rate and the output level is made through the appreciation of the local currency which, by creating a current account deficit, brings about a rise in foreign exchange assets and thus in output.

11. Formally, the impact of a change in nominal credit on the inflation rate, the output level and the balance of payments, respectively, are the following:

    $$dy/d\delta D = y_1[\Phi/(1+\Phi \cdot y_1(1+a_1))] > O$$
    $$d\delta P/d\delta D = \Phi/(1+\Phi \cdot y_1(1+a_1)) > O$$
    $$d\delta R/d\delta D = [(y_1 - c_1 y_1 - i_1 y_1) \Phi/(1+\Phi \cdot \Phi y_1(1+a))] - 1 < O$$

12. Leff and Sato (1980) and Blejer and Khan (1984) have shown empirically that a positive, significant correlation between banking credit and investment exists for a good number of developing countries. For industrialized countries, Jafee and Stiglitz (1988) come to the conclusion that 'investment may depend less on the interest rate charged than on the availability of credit'.

13. Formally, the impact of a credit contraction on the interest rate, the output level and the balance of

payments performance are, respectively, the following:

$$d\delta P/d\delta D = (1/A)[..(h_2+1)(c_1+i_1)-(z_1+1)h_2] > \text{and} < O$$
$$dy/d\delta D = (1/A)[h_2+h_1c](c_2+i_2) < O$$
$$\delta R/d\delta D = \{(1/A)(1+c_1+i_1((h_2+h_1c(c_2+i_2))\} + (c_2+i_2) > \text{and} < O$$
$$\text{with } A = [h_1(-a_1)] - (1-..a_1) < O$$

14. This interdependency between short and long term goals also appears when studying the microeconomic consequences of a credit contraction. Not all companies face the same credit constraint, thus a change in credit supply will not affect them in the same way. Therefore, not only will a general change in the price level take place (through the aggregate supply/demand mechanism described above), but a change will also occur in the relative prices of different sectors.

6 Stabilization policy: vision, reality, responsibility

by Grzegorz Kolodko

The crisis syndrome which now reaches beyond the economicsphere, to embrace also social and political institutions, presents a serious challenge to both policy and science, specifically - to economic sciences. Science is often held liable for adverse social and economic developments (consequently also for political events). One thus comes to ask, to what extent the level of theoretical knowledge and scientific postulates with regard to social and economic policy share the joint liability for crisis phenomena and processes. Is science keeping abreast of the challenges of development processes and proving its usefulness? Is policy willing and able to use the wisdom that science proposes? Answering these questions is worth a try, especially in view of accelerated changes taking place in the socialist countries at the turn of the eighties and nineties.

The general crisis of the socialist economy

Socialist economy bequeathed a general crisis. This is no business cycle recession due to an adverse combination of events and consisting in the appearance of unfavourable trends in the process of macroeconomic reproduction, but a wholesale crisis of economic, social and political relations, along with their concurrent institutions.

The general crisis of the socialist economy appears in three planes: systemic, structural and political. Attempts at overcoming it must therefore also consist in fundamental transformations in all these planes. Comprehensive and radical economic reform is the

79

answer to the systemic crisis. Attempts are made to counter the structural crisis with far reaching structural transformations, while a re-evaluation with regard to former objectives and means and methods used thus far, are the reaction to the crisis of economic policy.

It is clear that the extent of crisis phenomena differs from one postsocialist country to another. Without getting involved in the subtleties of definitions and methodology, we can say that the crisis syndrome is most obvious in Poland. Poland however is an exception not with this respect. What is exceptional, is the spectacular scale of crisis phenomena in so many areas (e.g. inflation, shortages, foreign debt, environmental pollution, depreciation of the ethos of work, ideological chaos and others), much broader than in other countries.

Much progress has been achieved in the recent years, both in socialist and Western literature, with regard to the theoretical explanation of crisis phenomena in post socialist economies. It can be attributed to the - unfortunately - increasing amount of empirical material and a more scientific approach to the subject matter. On the one hand, I specifically refer to the fact, that apologetics often practised in the days of socialism is being very quickly shelved. On the other, primitive Sovietology in Western literature is losing ground to an ever richer professional literature. Advances in these areas hardly mean that unanimity has been reached on the sources, essence and the consequences of the general crisis of socialism. Conversely, there are even more differences, if one also considers the ways of overcoming this crisis.

Science and policy

Joan Robinson once said that an economist's answer is a politician's question. Much as it tempting, this is a passive approach. One must ask the question about the origin of such important divergences between the postulates of economic science (in their normative function) and the decisions of economic policy.

First, science is imperfect and one must admit that there are even fundamental questions to which it may have no answers at a given time. Second, its answers may not be readily applicable and thus may be useless for practical purposes. Third, economic sciences are not, and will probably never be - ideologically and politically neutral. This is why there may often be many answers to a single question and it cannot be always unequivocally determined where the objective truth lies. Fourth, politicians are often unwilling or incapable of using scientific achievements. Fifth, economic postulates (especially in times of deep crisis) may be sheer demagogy in disguise, usurping the name of science, which may turn policy away from science as such, or build policy on demagogy and make science responsible. Sixth, policy often strives to instrumentalize research, incapacitating science and leading to scientific servility. Seventh, science may put forward rational solutions, that policy will readily apply, but the economy, and a population unwilling to bear the necessary therapy, thus making them unenforceable. Eighth, science is not infallible, especially on society and economy.[1] It deserves being stressed here, that spreading economic and political destabilization - is hardly helpful in enhancing the influence of science on policy and thus - on social and economic reality, insofar as the latter is a function of policy rather than of spontaneous processes. While one may observe an increased interest of policy in science, reflected, among other things, in impatient questions asked of science, there are other, disturbing phenomena. I refer especially to spreading demagogy, mostly in the form of various 'miraculous' anti-crisis recipes, uncertainty as to the desired directions of development processes in the face of ever stronger political struggle and ideological chaos, and the unusually strong pressure of time. In connection with the last remark, one must stress the danger of scientific analyses and syntheses becoming more superficial, of theory becoming journalistic or even confusion of theory with ideology.

Dogmatism represents a special threat to the proper development of economic sciences and their application. Unfortunately, it is not only difficultto shed its yoke but, what is more, one can observe a propensity for extreme attitudes with this respect. Negative experiences with one economic system or policy tend to lead to extreme attitudes and to the overrating of radically opposed systems. Such extreme attitudes are to be observed in both science and policy, and their relationship is obvious. Quite naturally the general crisis of socialism diverted the interest of economic sciences towards liberal theories. However, what can be called an explosion of these theories, are often expressed in the rather in discriminate adoption of various 'ultra market' programs or primitive monetarism, lacking even serious studies of Western literature.

While sympathizing with market and monitories trends in the structural and institutional transformations of the socialist economy, one should avoid taking extreme positions, especially on economic policy. This point is also emphasized with regard to the Mazowiecki government's economic Program (1989), which was precisely an example of such one sided espousal of scientific proposals. As a contemporary observer noted right upon its promulgation in the autumn of 1989. 'The authors' conviction that the market is the only admissible regulating mechanism and that the fullest possible elimination of the state from the economy sound (...) like a dogma. For it is hard to give another name to a situation where the implementation of a principle seems more important than the balance of losses and benefits derived therefrom.' (T. Jezioranski, 1989) The fundamental danger involved in such dogmas lies in a peculiar revival of wishful thinking. For attempts to transplant solutions proved in other institutional and structural environments, to a fundamentally different environment of a destabilized economy of shortage, are nothing but day dreaming.

Neither plan nor market system[2]

The plan versus market dilemma has been solved. This statement applies to the vast majority of the ex-socialist economies. In the Soviet Union, we can observe increasingly heated discussions typical of the period of naive faith (the early eighties in the case of Poland) in the chances of combining the advantages of central planning with the merits of market economy.[3]

The economic system inherited by the democratic governments is a curious hybrid. It combines the negative features of both planned and market system. Taking another approach, one might say that it is a neither plan, nor market system, a peculiar state of systemic vagueness, very threatening to economic performance. In such a situation, the crisis syndrome develops and becomes more acute. Crisis phenomena have been originally caused by a set of other reasons, but at a point where the old system no longer dominates, while the new has not yet set in, these causes are strong enough to sustain and fuel these destructive social and economic processes.

This was particularly visible in the phenomenon called shortageflation (Kolodko-McMahon 1987, Kolodko 1988). It consists in the parallel growth of both price and repressed (accumulation of excess money balances). inflation. The manifestations of this process have been increasingly strong in reformed socialist economies in the second half of the eighties, more recently also in Romania and Bulgaria. We observe an accelerating price inflation and more acute shortages in all the countries reforming rather than rejecting socialist structures. The more these countries delay the inevitable market and monetary reforms, the more dramatic will their future shortageflation be. This thesis is corroborated by Chinese and Soviet experiences.

Shortageflation has a special importance in this context. It is not merely a sum of the two types of inflationary processes, but a third, entirely new quality, which has a highly adverse impact on the process of social reproduction and hinders further progress in the implementation of institutional and structural changes. There is solid evidence to corroborate the statement that the shortageflation syndrome is the most painful consequence and also, the main threat to the process of economic and political reforms. Among other reasons, this view is based on the fact that market mechanisms are hardly possible to introduce in one stroke under such conditions.[4] Thus, although the outcome of the plan versus market dilemma in favour of the latter is obvious, one should not yield to naive neoliberal theories, typical of the laissez faire era. Introducing a market type regulation into the economy is a task for a whole generation. There is no doubt that many mistakes entailing grave consequences will be committed in the process, if time and societal requirements of the exercise are lost out of sight.

Interestingly, these mistakes are repeated in a similar sequence and ways by one country after another. This is demonstrated, among other things, in the approach to the establishment of the capital market in Hungary, then in Poland, by the experiences with the operation of employee selfmanagement confronted with the attempted expansion of market mechanisms (Yugoslavia /1965/, then Poland /1981/ later Hungary /1984/ and the Soviet Union /1987/) or in debates on the sources, essence and ways to overcome the inflationary overhang. Preceding the money confiscation of January 1991, Soviet debates of 1989-1990 sounded very much like earlier Polish deliberations. We find that economies and societies behave like people, especially the young and prefer to learn by their own trial and error!

Second Japan or second Argentina?

Economic crisis brings necessary adaptive action to the daily agenda. First comes economic stabilization, which in conjunction with the necessary measures in the systemic, structural and political planes, should assure relatively stable growth in the longer term. Comes the question about the nature of stabilizing and adaptive action, about the instruments of economic policy to be used in its course and lastly - about the possible economic, financial, social and political consequences.

Japan in the title is obviously an epitome. A second Argentina is much less of an epitome and I shall revert to that later. After all, looking maybe not for a standard to be copied, but for some point of reference for the visions of Poland's economic growth is quite natural.

The second reason to ask the question Japan or Argentina is connected with the declarations of some politicians, who claim to hold the advanced Western economies as their models,[5] suggesting thereby their naive faith that such models (and their development levels) can be within reach in a not too distant future, provided their systemic and political solutions are implemented. One may unfortunately have some very grave doubts with this respect, though there are other views on the subject which sound like fairy tales.[6]

The fundamental problem of a reformed economy, which is no longer centrally planned but not yet market regulated, is that it is extremely *difficult to initiate positive adaptive processes* precisely because of the lack of market-type regulation. One actually faces a series of negative adjustments, which fuels shortageflation mentioned earlier, bearing adversely the market oriented economic reform. For example, it is hardly by chance that we failed to attain a *positive real interest rate*, although interest rates have been raised many times in the recent years. This simply cannot be done under the conditions of rising inflation and acute shortages (Kolodko 1989c).

We can take another example, that it is the insufficient liberalization of prices that is the main cause of persisting shortages. Actually, this problem is much more complex, because with shortageflation and the lack of an adequately developed financial and banking sector, compounded by the closed character of the national economy, *liberalizing prices alone*, without taking other necessary measures, which sometimes require many years to implement, *will only produce ever higher cost, price and income levels.* We must emphasize here, contradicting naive liberal theories, that it is the companies that are not interested or willing to raise their prices to the ceilings set by demand, because it is easier for them to operate in a market with excess demand. Topinski (1989 p. 31) is right to stress that '...there is no evidence to confirm the relationship between the acuteness of shortages and the intensity of administrative price controls'.[7]

These comments were intended to corroborate the thesis that if a postsocialist economy in a deep crisis is set entirely free, to operate only by the market rules, many *negative adjustment processes* may be initiated and this may lead to intensification of crisis phenomena, rather than to their elimination. Parallel to that, we have previously unknown negative phenomena and processes, such as unemployment. Hence, more analogies fitting especially the Polish economy at the turn of 90s are to be found in the Latin American countries.

These analogies have been observed by a Swedish journalist, who wrote: 'Many freshly baptized "advocates of the free market economy" in the ranks of the former opposition put too much faith in the trouble-free relationship between the market and democracy, usually derived from superficial observations of advanced Western societies, rather than from comparisons of Polish reality with Chile or Turkey, which would have been more appropriate.' (*Dagens Nyheter* 6th July 1989) Unfortunately, one must basically agree with this view. It is therefore worthwhile to have a look at what has been going on in countries resembling Poland, for we should know how to draw the right conclusions from these historical experiences.

The *Chilean* economy embarked on its stabilization effort under martial law, imposed after the overthrow of Allende's democratically elected government in the autumn of 1973. Thus, adjustment processes took place when democratic institutions were suspended. After nearly a decade of such efforts, inflation was brought down to the psychological barrier of 10 per cent. However, this was paid for with a very strong differentation is the population's living standards, which actually drove an important part of the society into poverty. Among other things, it was also connected with huge unemployment, which peaked with 21 per cent in 1982. A very deep recession was another cost paid for a neoliberal adjustment policy. Industrial output in 1982 fell by as much as 25 per cent in comparison with the 1973 level, there was a dramatic decline in domestic savings (and consequently - investment) and rapid rise in foreign debt service (Lin 1987). Only after these dramatic stabilization and adjustment processes did the Chilean economy enter the growth stage, which wasn't trouble-free either. Hence, Chile's 'economic miracle' is another myth, because it was paid for with nine years of huge costs and deprivations (which would have probably been unacceptable to the society if it weren't for the dictatorship).

Chilean stabilization took place in three stages. The first between September 1973 and the summer of 1976 consisted mostly in fiscal and monetary restrictions imposed in order to stabilize the economy. The second, lasting from June 1976 to June 1979 featured attempts to use the exchange rate as a means of stabilizing inflation (Edwards 1984). Lastly, the third stage between June 1979 and June 1982 which efforts were made to follow a passive monetary policy combined with a constant exchange rate of the peso to the US $. It is worth noting here, that it is then that the notion of *hyperstagflation* was formed by Ramos (1980) as the most accurate description for Chile's situation in that period.

Argentina's experiences with stabilization and adjustment measures should have inspired even more caution. Efforts made by President Carlos Menem immediately after he took power in summer 1989 would have succeeded, provided there had been sufficient foreign support to stabilize the currency. This time, the early effects of stabilization measures were more promising than ever before. However, the stabilization effort failed again in late 1989, when - after a sharp devaluation - the monthly rate of inflation has soared back to over 50 per cent.

The history of Argentina's stabilization measures could be divided into many chapters and sub-chapters. One can point to two of them in the seventies. The first, covering the period between March 1976 and December 1978, involved successive attempts at various liberalization programs,[8] designed as panacea to the crisis and hyperinflation. In the second phase (January 1978 - March 1981) attempts were made to check inflation with the exchange rate policy. However, these efforts failed. Inflation was stabilized only temporarily and it was followed by a new hyperinflation (Calvo 1983, Kolodko 1987). In 1982, that is six years after these liberalization attempts, the GDP in real terms was still 1.2 per cent lower than in 1985, while industrial output crashed over that period by as much as 39 per cent. What is more, foreign debt kept on rising. By the end of the decade it stood at 60 billion US $ and the per capita figure was much higher than in Poland. Argentina's export industries however, are better developed than Poland's.

Further attempts at stabilization failed. The socalled 'Austral Plan', consisting in monetary reform launched early in the second half of the last decade failed too (Machinea and Fanelli 1989). Argentina's economy was plunged in hyperinflation and economic stagnation.

If however, we look at measures taken in the framework of stabilization initiated in the second half of 1989, it must be emphasized that Argentina has a relatively developed though highly inefficient financial sector (including banking) and a capital market, both operating in a market environment. This is not the case postsocialist economies. These remarks notwithstanding, one should remember that Poland's situation resembles Argentina's more closely than that of any of the advanced Western economies. One must realize that Argentina has a per capita GNP of 2.390 US $, while Poland, according to the same estimates (World Development Report 1989, World Bank, p. 165) - only US $ 1.930. The main problem thus, is that a 'second Argentina', would hardly be an extremely bad option for Poland - implying a catching up from current levels.

Imagination and responsibility

Nowadays, economic sciences and policy need imagination more than ever before. There is an urgent need to elaborate more extensive warning forecasts and for policy to use them. These are forecasts 'which are sure not to come true, but which point to the need to combat trends which are bound to appear unless countered' (Karpinski 1989, p. 25).

It has to be admitted: science often fails to provide satisfactory answers to challenges it is faced with. In such cases, it is only natural that people draw on solutions tested elsewhere. This is partial explanation of the yearning to draw on the achievements of the most advanced countries. This yearning is justified to some extent, like it is justified to observe the experiences of countries which have different economic systems, but similar development levels.

This is why comparative studies, in at least three planes, are particularly important at the present stage. First, in comparison to the experiences of other post socialist economies (especially of China, of Hungary, of Vietnam and of East German provinces). Second, particularly interesting are less advanced countries, especially those with a high share of the public sector on the one hand and suffering from serious social and economic destabilization on the other. Third and last, it is necessary to follow the experiences of advanced market economies, especially those with a high share of the public sector. One should however avoid indiscriminate transplantation of elements from these experiences to the conditions of a destabilized post-socialist economy.

Science like policy calls for much imagination, which should facilitate the screening of various proclaimed theses and contemplated measures. If we follow the debates on the successive Polish stabilization programs, starting with the government program for curbing inflation in the years 1983-1985 (Program 1983) to the economic Program (1989), it becomes obvious that imagination is in short supply. This is hardly a specific feature of Polish economy and policy, because these remarks may well apply to Latin American countries. Economic destabilization and the pressure of time leads to radically sounding but hasty measures, taken without due consideration in both cases - thus the outcomes can hardly differ so much.

This lack of imagination is frequently related to the strong pressures exerted on economic policy. We can take the example of the indexation of salaries in Poland in 1989 or the socalled 'marketization' of the agriculture. It wasn't all that difficult to anticipate the hyperinflationary threat stemming therefrom (Kolodko 1989b) and yet it was ignored because of the servile attitude of a part of the scientific society and the short-sighted docility of economic policy.

Given contemporary economic trends and stabilization measures, there was no doubt that Poland was threatened with a combination of exceedingly adverse processes in the 1990s: a rise in overall price levels reaching a scale typical of hyperinflation, an even deeper economic recession accompanied by mass unemployment and growing foreign debt. In other terms: shortageflation turns into slumpflation, i.e. a secular trend of decay.

Different criteria can be used to appraise the situation in the end of the eighties, but it would be difficult to view it as more favourable than in the beginning of the decade. Output was still below the 1979-1982 recession levels. The net distributed national income in 1989 reached only 95 per cent of the 1978 figure and foreign debt had more than doubled since then. Consumption per capita before the drastic shock treatment has not yet recovered to the level of the explosive year of 1980, while investment in real terms was lower by about one third than a decade ago. Inflation was many times higher (12.5 per cent was the average annual rate in the years 1979-1981).

Remarks made by D.M. Nuti during the previous recession of the Polish economy are particularly meaningful in view of the above comparisons: 'If Poland were a capitalist country in a similar crisis, painful but fairly automatic processes and policy responses would be set in motion. There would be hyperinflation, currency devaluation, drastic public expenditure cuts and deflationary taxation measures, tight money, high interest rates, divestment, bankruptcies and plant closures, and a couple of million unemployed. Some external creditors would get very little, or nothing at all, following the financial collapse of their debtors; some of the remaining debt would be offset by the sale to foreigners of financial assets (shares, bonds), land, building and plant. Fresh external finance would be available to the more credible borrowers. Unemployment would keep the unions in check, restraining real wages and ensuring labour discipline. The drop in real wage trends and industrial streamlining would eventually promote exports and encourage new investment, attracting foreign capital; *in ten years or so the economy would be getting out of the crisis*'. (Nuti 1982, p. 47; bold print by GWK). This scenario hasn't yet come true for obvious reasons. One should however not forget about the ways and impact of some stabilizing and adaptive mechanisms in a different systemic environment.

This is why extraordinary caution should be advised with regard to realignment on market and monetary solutions, which may be right as to the directions, but may bring, as has often been the case in economic and social processes, quite different effects than promised. Given these remarks, one cannot fail to ask whether the promise of 1 percent of monthly inflation by mid 1990 stemmed from the lack of imagination or of responsibility?

Looking at a somewhat different angle, it is worthwhile to note the lag between scientific postulates and political decisions. Michal Kalecki, drawing on his experience as adviser, and not only to Polish governments, used to say that it is not true that politicians don't take economists' advice; they do but that applies to the economists of the

87

past generation. One could now add that taking the advice of the coming generation may be equally inappropriate insofar as their advice may apply their visions of the future, rather than to present day reality.

Given the determinants and relationships discussed above, one may well fear that overcoming the general crisis of socialist economy and the transition to a modern and civilized market economy will be a lengthy and complex process. Scientific cognition of the subject is rather poor, though there is no doubt that much progress has been achieved in the recent years. Naturally, it is the countries in deepest crisis and with most destabilized economies that seem to have most achievements in this area.

The road to stabilization will probably lead through further destabilization. As Professor Czeslaw Bobrowski once said: 'Questions and problems facing us multiply in geometrical progression, while our knowledge about the ways to overcome them - in arithmetical progression'. Still the lack of time cannot be an explanation for the lack of professionalism which can sometimes be observed, for spreading demagogy and the servility of science to the authorities, whatever they may be.

Notes

1. Pajestka (1989, p. 171) gives an interesting presentation of this problem. Asking questions '...why was a mechanism which did not prove itself in practice adopted as socialist and why has it operated for so long without necessary adaptation, he states: The first element of the answer is that science is conceited, and believes its own infallibility. This fallacy needs no comprehension nor should it be directed exclusively at Marxism. (...) man became fascinated with science, showing less than normal human caution, which tends to critically evaluate everything and to be very careful in the formulation of conclusions (...) The blindness of mankind, believing without reserve that science shows the right way and that it should be fully trusted, is proper to that stage of human civilization in which man became fascinated with himself, with his "divine" qualities. I do not mean to say here that science should not be trusted, but that it should not be trusted indiscriminately. Moreover, the more difficult are the processes under consideration, the harder it is to relate them to real experiences and the more caution is advisable.'

2. This term was first used by Bauer (1984), later becoming part of the standard Eastern European economic vocabulary. /ed. note/

3. For more on non European socialist countries see, among others: W. Andreff (1989), D.S.G. Goodman (1989) and S.G. Roca (1989).

4. Without getting involved in the appraisal of particular systems regulating national economies, János Kornai (1990/c) is right to emphasize that the relationship between market-type regulation and state ownership is weak. Hence, it is difficult to expect market-type behaviour on the part of economic organizations without first introducing appropriate changes in ownership.

5. As an example, we might refer here to a statement by one of the then ministers of the Polish government, who treats Sweden as a point of reference and consequently believes we should follow its experiences. One should nonetheless remember that Sweden is more than a definite system and policy but also, most of all, a very high GNP level (15.5 thousand US $ per capita in 1988) and a modern economic structure. Even if we made the absurd assumption that Sweden should now go into secular stagnation and Poland - into an era of another economic miracle with a

constant annual GNP growth rate of 10 per cent per capita, we would still need 25 (!) years to have equal economic development levels.

6. During a debate entitled 'We are sentenced to optimism' M. Krassowski asked: 'Let's assume that the market is already there. In ten years from now, will we be closer to West Germany or Peru?' J. Korwin-Mikke replied: 'West Germany will be very easy to leave behind'. Vid. *Odrodzenie* 1989, No. 40, p. 6.

   Interestingly, a year after the famous shock treatment nearly a quarter of Polish voters followed the man of the moment, Tyminski, running on a fairly similarly sounding election platform. This is indicative of the lasting presence of this body of opinion in Poland (editorial note).

7. For more on experiences with price controls see, among others: J.K. Galbraith (1952) and H. Rockoff (1984).

8. Interestingly, politicians often assume that this time it will really be the decisive attempt. It is usually otherwise. The spectacular case of Bolivian stabilization of the second half of the eighties is frequently invoked in Poland (without remembering its enormous cost, among other things, the doubling of the unemployment rate from 10% to 20%). It is worth adding, that the Bolivian case involved six successive stabilization and adjustment programs over three years, implemented by seven successive ministers of finance and seven central bank governors.

Part IV
Systemic Change and Stabilization:
external conditions

7 Unresolved issues of Comecon trade in convertible currencies

by Gábor Oblath

Introduction

This Chapter addresses some of the controversial issues related to switching over to hard currency payments in trade among Eastern European countries. It focuses on the Hungarian-Soviet case and treats the problems from a Hungarian perspective.

It has to be stressed that the reference to the 'Hungarian perspective' does not mean that the views expressed would in any way represent official Hungarian opinion. This reference simply implies that it is mainly from the point of view of macroeconomic effects on the Hungarian economy that the issues are discussed below. First, the unresolved issues of the switchover are discussed. Second, the Soviet interests involved are treated. Third, costs and benefits of the swithover for Hungary are surveyed. The last section treats the prospects and possible dangers related to the new payments system.

It should be noted that the present chapter indents to discuss perspectives and expectations related to the switch over *preceding* the actual implementation of the new payments system. This analysis, however, might be more than of mere historical interest, since the open questions, unclarified issues are likely to remain relevant for quite some time after the switchover.

What does trade in hard currency mean?

In March 1990, representatives of the Soviet and Hungarian governments agreed to break with the existing transferable rouble (TR) payments system and switchover to hard currency (dollar) payments in their economic relations, beginning 1991. As a part of this agreement, the partners agreed to convert some 0.8 billion TR Hungarian claims on the USSR to dollars at a rate of 0.92 $/TR.

However, some basic questions related to the switchover in the payments system have not been clarified. In what follows I wish to treat two of these basic issues. First: what is the institutional system underlying the new payments system? Second: what is the actual character of 'hard currency payments'?

The major question related to *the institutional system* touches the role of the state (government agencies) and that of enterprises, respectively, in conducting trade relations. In the traditional framework of CMEA trade, transactions are based on a system of intergovernmental agreements involving socalled government obligations for buying and selling certain amounts of specific goods specified in the agreements. In this system companies are considered to be simply the executioners of central decisions. The logic of these trade arrangements reflects the workings of the traditional central planning system.

However in the Hungarian case, where, since 1968,significant changes have been implemented in the domestic economic system, the pure logic sketched above could not be maintained in the country's CMEA relations. Due to the enlarged autonomy of enterprises, a mixed-up situation emerged. In this government agencies took decisions affecting microeconomic agents in contrast with the intentions of the Hungarian reform of 1988. Meanwhile enterprises were also in a position to initiate and even force the authorities to take certain decisions including international government obligations, irrespective of their final macroeconomic implications (e.g significant trade surplus or the large scale subsidization of exports). According to many experts[1], this state affairs in the country's CMEA trade was in itself a major obstacle to introducing fully fledged market relations in the Hungarian economy. The logic and consequences of central planning were always present and reinforced in Hungary, due to the importance of foreign trade relations with CMEA countries (representing still more than 40 per cent in Hungarian foreign trade, even in 1989, after years of decline in this trade).

Taking a look at the switchover in the payments system from this angle, one of the major question seems to be whether the discontinuation of payments in transferable roubles is accompanied with a break with the above mentioned aspects of the state trading system.

If so, Hungary's trade relations with her major Eastern partner, the Soviet Union, could transform in a fundamental way. Companies, at least on the Hungarian side, could take charge of trading with the USSR, just as with other countries. This would, however,entail significant short run costs to be discussed later.

If the system of state trading were maintained, the switchover to dollar payments would not make much sense from Hungary's point of view. It would simply entail significant short term costs (although lower than in the first case) without, however, longer term benefits.

Switching over to convertible payments *may imply three basically different actual practices* in trade among East European countries. First, it may mean *effective* (or real) *hard currency* payments; second, an interstate *clearing system* in which the unit of account and that of payments is denominated in a convertible currency (most likely in dollars); and third, an inter-enterprise *barter system* in which prices are expressed in hard currency (dollar).

Effective hard currency payments imply that the standards relevant in international payments would apply to trade between Hungary and the Soviet Union.

Cash payments and commercial credits (under terms similar to international ones) would be applied. The two countries, or more precisely, trading agents of the two countries, would not be different from each countries' point of view from any other (Western) trading partner. Evidently, this solution would comply most clearly with the basic changes in the institutional system discussed above.

A *dollar clearing system* may mean two rather different solutions. *First*, it might involve a simple renaming of the present system (i.e. naming the unit of account as 'dollar', rather than TR) with everything in the institutional system left unchanged. The only change that would take place in this case, is the one to be discussed below: the deterioration of Hungary's bilateral terms of trade with the Soviet Union.

Second, dollar clearing might involve an agreement to regularly pay the balances in effective convertible currencies;[2] in this case the economic consequences of a clearing arrangement could come quite close to those of effective hard currency payments.

However, it is important to note that both types of clearing arrangements assume that the central government in the Soviet Union is in a position to undertake obligations to sell and buy certain products, and that the government of the USSR is in a position to actually enforce its decisions and international agreements within the Soviet economy.

A third solution might be a system of inter-enterprise *barter arrangements* in which dollars (hard currencies) would have no other role but being the unit of account in which prices are determined. In spite of the fact that neither partner openly promotes - moreover the USSR explicitly restricts - this solution, willy-nilly it might become the framework of a significant portion of trade denominated in hard currency.

Interests on the Soviet side

A reasonable starting point for assessing the intentions related to the switchover on the Soviet side seems to be that 'Soviet interests' (or intentions) *as such* do not exist. In contrast to the situation prevailing a few years ago, when reference to 'Soviet interests' unmistakably meant the interests of central authorities of the USSR, nowadays it is far from easy to determine what 'Soviet interests' imply. The interests of the central government, its agencies (ministries having received foreign trading rights), and of traditional foreign trade organizations are rather different. Local interests (those of governments of the republics and companies within these republics) might, again, be rather different concerning relations with Hungary under the new payments system.

One point, however, seemes to be quite clear. Namely, that in the Soviet Union there has been a sense of 'being cheated', i.e. having to tolerate unfavourable terms of trade with the CMEA countries, due to the relative undervaluation of Sovietenergy and raw material exports to, and overpricing of manufactured imports from, Eastern Europe.[3] An important factor underlying the Soviet decision to promote the switchover to dollar payments and the application of world market prices certainly seems to have been the intention of turning around the terms of trade in the USSR's favour.

Turning to practical matters, while central organs wish to increase their power and authority, the country's real production is declining. Therefore, resources *under the control* of the central government of the USSR is likely to diminish in the foreseeable future. As an important consequence of these trends, what the central organs can offer and demand is not necessarily a reflection of the supply and demand conditions of the USSR with respect to Hungary. Potential supply (demand) towards (from) Hungary might be larger than what is conceived, and expressed, by central organs. However, since at present the major part of the production in the USSR is still under central control, it does matter a lot what the interests related to the switchover of central organs are.

There are *three* possible intentions at the central level on the Soviet side which might result in a collision of Soviet and Hungarian interests.

The *first* possibility is implementing a new payments system with an unchanged institutional system of trading relations. This implies a larger volume of Hungarian exports because of the terms of trade loss - to be discussed below. A dollar clearing system, i.e. renaming the transferable rouble to dollars and capturing the terms of trade gains would serve those interests most fully.

Second, the central organs in the USSR might wish to achieve the largest possible net dollar revenues as a consequence of the switchover. Due to the liquidity problems of the Soviet Union, this option can not be ruled out as unrealistic. The implementation of effective dollar payments would serve these interests most fully.

Third, as an extreme possibility, central organs in the Soviet Union might aim at capturing both of the above mentioned benefits: a larger volume of imports accompanied by large net dollar revenues from Hungary. This could be achieved if Hungarian exports (mainly machines) were sold under the terms of commercial credits - the demand for them would increase under these terms - while energy and raw material exports of the Soviet Union would have to be paid for in cash. An effective dollar payment system would be well suited to serve such endeavors.

Keeping in mind these possible intentions on the Soviet side, in the following we shall try to asses (both the short and longer run) effects of the switchover under various actual payments arrangements.

Effects of the switchover under alternative payment regimes

Although the switchover is certain to involve costs under any of the above discussed payments systems, the short termcosts are likely to be higher if *effective convertible payments* are applied.

The direct negative effects of the switchover are related to changes in the foreign trade on the one hand and to sizable losses of budgetary revenues, on the other. *The indirect* effects concern the possible decline of production, increase in unemployment and in the domestic price level.

As for *foreign trade*, three direct effects, namely those on the prices, the volume and the structure of trade are expected. The combination of these is likely to result in a large negative impact on the trade balance.

Expected *changes in export and import prices* indicate a significant deterioration in the terms of trade. Depending on methods of, and assumptions behind the various calculations, estimates concerning the negative change in the commodity terms of trade vary between 20 and 30 per cent. At this point it is worth giving a brief summary of an investigation, conducted in 1989 with the participation of the present author, aimed at clarifying the possible terms of trade effect of the transition. This survey relied on both statistical data and expert opinion; it applied direct comparison of actual transferable rouble (TR) foreign trade prices on the one hand and actual or expected dollar prices, on the other. It, therefore, avoided the pitfalls involved in previous similar attempts that used exchange rates (including the unrealistic and irrelevant official rate TR/USD) when trying to asses the terms of trade effect of the switch over. The method of the investigation was the following: representative products of major exporting and importing branches were selected and both expert opinion and objective data were used to estimate what the potential dollar export (import) prices of these products were if traded for dollars with the Soviet Union. Objective data (price quotations from international markets) were used for sample products (oil, raw materials etc.) and expert opinion was requested for manufactured products. Based on this information USD/TR price relatives were determined for each product and, by weighting these, for the major exporting and importing industries, as well as for total exports to and imports from the USSR. The ratio of the price relative for total exports to imports indicated the "commodity terms of trade effect" of the transition; this turned out to be roughly 25 per cent terms of trade loss.

As for the structure of this loss, it results mainly from a 25% decline in the nominal price of machinery exports and a 90% increase in the price of metallurgy imports (i.e. machines sold for 1000 TR-s on average could be sold for USD 750 after the transition; metallurgical products bought for 1000 TR would have to paid for USD 1900). In other product groups relative price changes were less significant. It should, however, be borne in mind that these estimates were made before the increase in oil and other energy prices. Taking into consideration the latter, in early 1991 the expected commodity terms of trade loss due to the transition is estimated to be around 30 per cent; the resulting income loss might amount to 1300-1800 million dollars.[4]

Although there are several difficulties involved in determining the magnitude of possible terms of trade changes, the problems with estimating prospective volume changes are even larger. There is a controversy on this issue.

Some believe that lower export prices induce a larger demand for Hungarian products; while others expect that the Soviet demand will fall irrespective of price changes. The Hungarian supply is likely to respond to changes in Soviet demand. Butthere is a possibility that the Soviet Union decreases its imports in spite of the favourable price changes, while Hungarian capacities designed for exporting only to the Soviet market remain idle and will have to be closed down.

However, as mentioned above, there is some likelihood that Soviet purchases do not decrease very much or even increase; this would be the case if lower prices for Hungarian exports induce Soviet buyers to purchase more (or, at least, not to decrease imports) from Hungary. Commercial credits offered to the USSR could have similar effects. But because of theextremely large uncertainties surrounding the prospective regulation of foreign trade in the USSR, it is not really possible to assess ex ante the effects of the switchover on trade volumes.

In contrast to the difficulties surrounding estimates on the prospective volumes, forecasting changes in the *structure of trade* has seemed to be relatively easy. The USSR had been expected to import more consumer goods, agricultural products and foodstuffs; and less machines than previously as a this is a direct consequence of the state of the Soviet domestic market. The intentions of the Soviet authorities, revealed in early 1991 concerning the structure of imports from Hungary, cast some doubts on the assumptions. However without having hard facts on the Soviet demand for Hungarian imports under the new payments system, one can only conclude that the effects of the switchover on the structure of trade are ambiguous.

Be that as it may, the expected change in the terms, volume and structure of trade will certainly have a negative impact on the Hungarian state *budget* as well. This is so because in Hungary the domestic price of energy has been based on world market prices converted at the official exchange rate for the dollar (close to 65 Ft/$ in 1990). The difference between the former and the lower than world market TR import price converted at the ruling exchange rate

98

(27 forints/roubles) was simply taxed away. Therefore, the government in Hungary was a beneficiary of the difference between import prices from the Soviet Union and world market prices.

As far as exports are concerned, sales of machinery to the Soviet Union was taxed, while light industrial and agricultural (food) exports were subsidized. Therefore, the structural changes associated with the switchover are likely to increase the negative price effects on the budget. Estimates concerning the negative impact on the budget of the switch over vary between 30 to 70 billion forints (0.6 to 1 billion dollars).

Further costs related to the switchover concern spillover effects on the balance of trade with the West as well as domestic employment effects. As to the former, a negative impact on the Western trade balance can be expected, since many companies presently importing from the USSR plan to switch to Western imports. A part of Hungary's former Western trade that was based on reexporting, though in somewhat refined form, of items imported for TR (mainly oil products and chemicals) will become unprofitable. In this case it is only the value added that can be considered as a loss. A further part of the turnover was accounted and paid in dollars until now between Hungary and the Soviet Union, in which Hungary had a surplus. This will become a part of total trade - decreasing Hungary's net exports to the West, but at the same time diminishing the negative impact of the switchover on the previous TR trade between Hungary and the USSR.

The switchover is likely to have a negative effect on *employment* in Hungary, through the possible decrease of sales to the Soviet Union and the latter's negative multiplier effects. Given the uncertainties surrounding changes in export volumes, any estimate on employment effects should also be extremely uncertain.

The switchover to effective hard currency payments can, however, have *several benefits* as well, most of which will be experienced only in the medium and long run. The most important long run benefit would stem from having the same kind of trade with the Soviet Union as with any foreign country. In the short term, the following positive impacts can be expected:

- First, and most important, Western companies wishing to reach the Soviet market would have an incentive to invest in Hungary. A lot of expertise has been accumulated on the ways and means of selling to the Soviet market in Hungary; many Hungarian firms have been involved in this activity. After switching to dollar payments, this expertise (as well as sales networks) could become an advantage for Western investors.
- Second, the behaviour of Hungarian companies selling to the Soviet market would change. Instead of being involved in bargaining with Hungarian government agencies, they would be forced *to perform* at the Soviet, as at any other market.
- Third, a special kind of supply constraint related to

99

imports from the 'rouble trade area' would be removed. Many products previously bought from the West would be available from the East as well; probably even at a lower price.

- Forth, an extremely difficult task for the Hungarian authorities, the restriction of exports to the USSR, in order to avoid the accumulation of unsustainable clearing surpluses in bilateral trade with the USSR, would become unnecessary.

If a *pure intergovernmental clearing arrangement* were applied, the volume of Hungarian exports would surely *increase*, since the deterioration in the terms of trade would have to be paid in kind, rather than in cash. The effects of this type of adjustment would *reinforce the dependence* of Hungary's manufacturing industry on the Soviet market, whose standards significantly depart from those of the world market.

What is worse, the Soviet Union, as discussed above, is increasingly becoming an unreliable partner. Therefore, obligations undertaken by the central organs in the USSR can no more be treated as certain. The dangers involved in clearing transactions are also related to the possible inability of the Soviet government to enforce already agreed exports.

The basic problem with dollar clearing arrangements is that they might involve an unchanged institutional system with worse terms of trade for Hungary with the USSR. A *modified clearing*, involving regular mutual hard currency payments could comeclose to an effective convertible payments system. In normal conditions this could be advocated as a transitory solution between the traditional TR system and the new hard currency payments arrangement.However, since the economic situation in the Soviet Union is far from being normal, this solution can be treated only with reservations. The major problem stems from the fact that the central authorities are not really in charge. Thus not just the 'obligation' to supply specific commodities can not be reliedupon, but intergovernmental obligations to pay at certain intervals can not be taken very seriously either.

Finally, inter-enterprise *barter agreements* might turn out to be a rather significant part of the trade between the two countries. There is nothing basically wrong with barter transactions; if their share increases, it implies that there is a scope for mutually beneficial transactions. The problems come only if the Hungarian government wishes to establish specialized large organizations ('trading houses') for conducting barter trade with the USSR. This might imply that Hungarian exports that could be sold to the USSR for dollars would become parts of global barter agreements, quite similarly to the arrangements of the previous system. But it is exactly this type of system that could, and indeed should, be replaced when switching over to dollar payments.

Prospects and dangers of the switchover

The most significant positive effect of the switchover is that Hungary could start to enter into real *trade* with the Soviet Union, based on comparative advantages. Political considerations involved in this trade could be replaced by economic ones.

This kind of a transformation with Hungary's major trading partner could lead to significant changes in the behaviour and strategies of Hungarian economic agents. The inevitable reorientation to other markets would be strongly induced, while mutually advantageous transactions with the East would not be hindered. An other result of the switchover might be psychological, but this could lead to consequences in the real economy: neither of the countries involved in this trade would feel cheated, as they presently do.

The switchover involves *dangers* as well, some of which have already been discussed above.

The most serious one stems from the possibility that the actual details in domestic regulation of Soviet trade with Central and Southeast Europe do not change in line with the political agreements reached with these countries. As a result, Hungarian companies wishing to export to the USSR, and Soviet companies willing to buy from Hungary, might have difficulties in arriving at mutually advantageous deals. This would be an unhappy, but not really likely, outcome, since it could mean that the gains from the new payments system would not be captured by the Hungarian partners, while the potential gains from the new type of trading arrangements could not be realized by the Soviet Union either.

The second danger is related to the possibility that both partners wish to maintain a strict clearing system denominated in dollars - this would imply that Hungarian companies could increase their exports to the USSR, while the necessary changes in the institutional system would not take place.

The third danger is related to a major terms of trade shock, involving a large deterioration in the bilateral or the overall hard currency trade balance. The income loss, as indicated above is estimated to be 1.3-1.8 billion dollars or 4.5-6.5 per cent of 1989 GDP. Although the trade balance effects of this income loss might be milder, this is an extremely serious blow to the Hungarian economy.[5] To cope with the negative trade balance effects, Western support is certainly required. The main justification of this assistance is that by switching over to convertible payments, Hungary's overall trade, just as that of other Eastern European countries, becomes a part of the global multilateral trade and payments system; this, however, involves transitory costs that, at least partly, call for outside financing. Switching over to convertible payments is a major step of this region on its road of integrating to the world economy. It would seem reasonable on the part of the West to support this endeavour.

What finally can be expected of the new payments regime in Eastern Europe? My forecast is that even after switching to dollar payments, a significant part of trade will remain under governmental surveillance. An important part of trade will be paid in effective dollars. It is most likely that the shore of barter arrangements will increase. Thus, *the new system is likely to be a mixed one*, in which the elements of all of the previous discussed arrangements will be involved. Arriving to a pure and simple hard currency payments system will take substantial time.

Hungarian economic policy will meet significant constraints, while microeconomic agents are likely to face serious difficulties in the short run. But adjustments, both in macroeconomic policies and at the micro level, to challenges resulting from the switchover should have positive effects in the medium and longer run on the overall performance of the Hungarian economy, just as on those of other Eastern European countries.

Notes

1. See Köves (1990), Köves-Oblath (1989), Szamuely, ed. (1989).
2. This would come close to the system applied in Finno-Soviet trade in the year 1990 (see Kivilahti and Rautava, 1990). The peculiarities of trade between Finland and the USSR are discussed in Oblath and Pete (1986).
3. This notion was picked up in the Western literature on CMEA trade as well, and referred to as 'implicit subsidization of Eastern Europe' by the Soviet Union. (Marrese-Vanous, 1983). The idea was strongly criticized (see e.g. Csaba, 1990/a, Köves, 1983) on grounds of leaving out of consideration the serious *costs* to Eastern Europe of its apparent 'subsidization'.
4. For further details see Oblath-Tarr (1991) and The World Bank (1991).
5. See also KOPINT-DATORG (1990)

8 The role of Western capital in the transition to the market - a systems' theoretical perspective

by Raimund Dietz

Ludwig von Mises (1920) was quite right in his claim that a fully collectivized economy would be unable to evaluate economic activities and was therefore doomed to perish. Economic calculation, according to Mises, is tied to exchange economy. This dictum has meanwhile been unequivocally confirmed by history, yet a theoretical basis appears still to be missing - as witness the inconclusive controversy on socialism (Lavoie 1985) Yet a theoretical foundation for that dictum was provided by the liberal philosopher Georg Simmel (1900/1990), in his 'Philosophie des Geldes' written originally between 1900 and 1907 - an opus that has been completely neglected by the economic theorists, even by the money theorists.[1] Simmel's text, however, dealt not with the failure of a planned economy, but with the theory of modern economic society, a theme that is of decisive importance especially for the postsocialist countries in their striving to reconstruct the market. Civil (free market) societies rest on *exchange communication*, according to Simmel.

We interpret the transition from a command economy to market economy as transition from bureaucratic command communication to exchange communication. During transition a systemic vacuum appears; it is ascribed to the discrepancy between the complex structure of an industrial society and as yet underdeveloped exchange communication. This discrepancy is responsible for the functional disturbances during transition (Section I). The systemic vacuum is characterized in the first place by the discrepancy between the advanced stage of material development and primitive communication (Section II). In Section III we present a theoretical concept, which serves as a base for the analysis. The central theses are: Exchange is the basic systems element, wherefrom very complex forms and structures are derived in an evolutionary way, such as money, prices, identities of organizations and markets. Exchange generates rationality of modern societies. From this follows the demand to set exchange communication into motion. In Section IV we pursue the question, on what level this can be done. Therein we discuss several avenues, which may well be followed simultaneously: the encouragement of small and medium size entrepreneurship; transformation of the state sector an opening of the economies; and, finally, the role of Western capital, which is to act as a heart pacemaker. Criteria are discussed in Section V which may help in assessing, which countries can expect faster transition. In Section VI we deal with the rank and place of the so called stabilization measures in transformation. Section VII considers the possibilities of compensating systemic deficiencies by means of undervaluing the currency and other price discounts. In the final section the author pleads for a political impulse for lessening investment risks and for eliminating investors' fears of taking the plunge. For sure it would be better to encourage Western investments than to deport East European immigrants.

From command to exchange communication

The transformation in Central and Eastern Europe and the USSR can be conceived as a transformation from command to exchange economies. This changeover is the change of the way by which society communicates in the economic subsystem. It is connected with a change of the logic, and in consequence, with the behavior of agents and with the material structure of the economy.

The logic of the command system is resource economics, i.e. a process of relating scarce material means to virtually infinite ends, where means and ends formulated in material terms are conveyed within a hierarchical structure. In consequence, scarcities appear as material constraints and the economy is a shortage economy (Kornai 1980). The logic of an exchange economy, in contrast, is the logic of an economy of private proprietors (owners), i.e. of a monetized capitalist economy. In a monetized economy it is money that ultimately governs the economic decisions. Before the selective resource constraint becomes effective, the monetary constraint takes effect. Thus money economies are slack economies (Riese 1990). While customers queue for goods in command economies, goods queue for customers in market economies. Also the entrepreneurial behavior is different. In centrally planned economies entrepreneurial behavior is 'paternalistic', the budget constraints are 'soft'. In exchange economies enterprises act autonomously and they are confronted by hard budget constraints. Their survival depends on earning a return on invested money, while the survival of enterprises in a planned economy depends on their subservience to superiors.

While market economies organize themselves (i.e. are autopoietic systems) by producing information on scarcities through the process of exchange, command systems lack internally produced information on scarcities and must imitate market economies (by relying, e.g., on prices generated on the real markets abroad). Due to this systemic deficiency are command economies systemically inferior to market economies.

Different systems produce different results. Infrastructure in command systems is usually underdeveloped, industry, in particular heavy industry, absorbs, or absorbed, too high a share of labour and capital. Services are generally neglected. Production is 'material intensive' (wasteful). Exports concentrate on energy, raw materials and semi-manufactures; prices per exported kilogram are very low. The transformation from the command to the exchange system (in political terms from a despotic to civil rule) boils down to the exchange of one communicative network for another.

Systemic vacuum in the postcommunist aftermath of Central and Southeastern Europe

The problem derives from the fact that in despotically organized societies the transition consists of two more or less separate phases: a phase in which the old system is being demolished and a phase in which the reconstruction of the civil society takes place. In between there comes into being a kind of no man's land: a *systemic vacuum*. It was expected by many that the transition from the network of a command economy - which was too primitive to master the complex problems of the modern world - to the network of exchange communication would automatically bring better results. These expectations are doomed to be disappointed since the phases are more or less separated, for the following five reasons.

1. *Despotic systems*, in our case the communist systems, defined themselves by and are based on the *negation and destruction of civil* socioeconomic *system*. Collective ownership presupposes the confiscation of private property, and central commands were secured by prohibition or at least inhibition of contracting (exchange). Thus the market may organize itself only after the demolition of the despotic rule.

An economy will function properly if its communications system is sufficiently complex to control the real system. The collapse of the command economies can be traced back to the violation of this rule: command systems are too primitive as to control efficiently complex industrial economies. However, with the dismantling of the command systems affairs do not improve but rather change for the worse, since the old and sick system is being phased away while the new system is not yet working.

Markets are to perform a very complex assignment in former communist countries from the very beginning: Central and East European economies are not primitive, they are, due to their degree of industrialization, highly complex worlds, which, in order to function, would require correspondingly complex communicative structures. We have learned from mainstream economics that an

105

imperfect market is a bad market. Oh, were it merely imperfect! The market, according to Hayek (1945), confirms its capabilities precisely in situations where there are imperfections (e.g. caused by non-homogeneous commodities). The markets in Central and East Europe are not only imperfect, they are in their infancy, comparable to the brain, far too small in relation to its bodily size, of a dinosaur: it is unable appropriately to control and steer the colossus it is meant to control. The task of the infant markets is much too voluminous and complex to be successfully tackled.

3. On the one hand the material structure of the real system is rather comprehensive. In order to function, highly industrialized economies must consist of elements all characteristic of Western economies. In a modern economy there cannot be any functioning product markets without functioning capital markets, no development of intra-industry trade without the mutual penetration of firms' assets, no internationalization of commerce without internationalization of capital.

On the other hand markets organize themselves upwards from below, i.e. from simple to ever more complex systems, thereby consuming *time*; the market is the evolutionary result of a long history. It started from modest cooperation between self-supporting units (families, tribes) and has extended its scope step by step by absorbing ever larger parts of production, and connecting ever more agents. Meanwhile it has established a worldwide network of exchange contacts between mutually fully dependent economic agents. For example, in order to compete on equal terms on product markets, a valuation of assets by the capital market is required, and, at the same time, a valuation of assets presupposes functioning product markets. It is this *simultaneity requirement* of good functioning product and capital markets that renders the marketization of the etatized economy so difficult.

4. Societal systems survive only if their participants find possibilities of continuing to communicate. This, according to the theorem of the socalled *double contingency* (Luhmann 1984), is always attended by risk. The risk of disruption of the stream of communication(s) during the period of transformation is higher, the probability of successive communicational events lower, for the economic logic of decisionmaking in command systems was very different from considerations prevailing in monetized modern economies. Thus arrangements between suppliers and customers, often imposed by decree, will only exceptionally meet the requirement of voluntary exchange. In addition, liberalization of the economies and their opening up to the world market may, no doubt, greatly expand the set of potential opportunities for trading. Meanwhile selection by the market will be more rigid, thus reducing the probability that any specific traditional relation can survive. Thus the network of purchases and sales will have to be tied almost from scratch.

5. Panta rei (everything is in flux), said an old Greek philosopher. Change is the principle of modern economies. However, due to the

106

heavily distorted structures of former socialist economies their material pattern are to be changed drastically. While the 'march' of the Eastern economies towards 'demanded' structures is very long, each single step on this march is more painful than in fully fledged market economies, since institutional devices to support these changes are lacking.

Constituents of a modern economic system

One of the decisive achievements of the 1989 revolution in Central and East Europe, is the fact that the aim of transformation is unmistakably identified. This is transformation into societies of Western, preferably West European type, along the lines of the welfare state. But whereas the aim is clear, the road is stony. This is because modern economic structures result from a lengthy evolutionary process, whereas the approach to that structure cannot be reproduced along the same evolutionary road. The existing structures in Central and Eastern Europe have long outgrown the potentialities of evolutionary change in the social organism.

Nevertheless it is necessary to have clear conception of how this evolution proceeds in modern capitalism. Relyingon Georg Simmel (1900/1990) and on the modern systems theory of Luhmann (1984, 1988) and Baecker (1988), I should like to indicate how the most complex structures in a modern society grow from simplest elements of *communication*. On this path 'up from below' the market presents itself as a system that produces information and that organizes and reproduces itself. Modern economies are, according to Luhmann (1988) 'autopoietic' (=selfcreating) systems.

According to Simmel (1900) *exchange is* the basic act of communication in a modern economy.[2] Exchange is a simple system element, wherefrom very complex forms and structures are derived, such as money, prices, modern private ownership, organizations. Conversely, the abolition of exchange communication and its replacement, e.g. through central commands, is connected with immeasurable economic and social consequences.

a) Whereas *mainstream economics* assumes known commodity spaces (defined by convex sets and the distribution of quantities) and practically excludes exchange communication,[3] *system theory* underlines that exchange actions constitute a prerequisite for making observation possible (Baecker 1988). This means that an offer to exchange must have been made to enable one to observe at what conditions something may be obtained. Other agents' preferences and production functions cannot be directly observed. One receives indications at the points of junction of the net of exchange communication. Without these the subjects act in a no man's land. Economies are constituting themselves only through exchange.

b) Having introduced money information concerning the degree of scarcities of goods is enormously simplified. Thereby the set of choices available is immeasurably enlarged. Thus money[4] is *the most productive social 'invention'*: only money enables man to shorten the long chain of technical connections, thereby dramatically easing his access to all goods, services and knowledge (Simmel 1900, p. 206). It is a prerequisite to fashioning out of a primitive society and 'extended order' (Hayek 1988). A change of money supply may be near neutral as affecting the real variables' structure; but money per se is anything but neutral. It is *the* medium that makes socialization possible.

c) Being the most general means of economic activity, money inevitably becomes the immediate target of human actions[5] (Simmel 1900, pp. 229). The producer/investor earns only to enlarge his payments potential (Luhmann 1988, pp. 131). Where the question is one of satisfaction of derived needs - and the more highly developed an economy, the more men depend on them - there the economy can only orient itself by reference to profit (as a price difference).

d) In a monetized economy all production factors are nothing but the material that is used by the selfaugmenting mechanism of value - represented by money as an accounting unit (Selbstvermehrung des Werts at Marx). In other words: the sphere of reality is harnessed to the reproduction process of money (better: capital) and thus *subsumed under the monetary sphere* (as its control sphere).

e) Exchange is a communicative act which *stands on its own;* i.e., its rationality needs neither justification from nor reference to other transactions. Subjects A and B exchange in the expectation that by exchanging they shall be better of. Voluntary exchange enhances both participants' welfare. On the other hand, a planning act p alludes to planning acts x, y, z etc. Its rationality is only secured if the activity triggered by p is reconciled with all the other consequences.

f) Thus, to avoid conflict among economic agents on the allotment of scarce resources, the center must have recourse to secrecy. Exchange, quite on the contrary, pacifies, competition is depersonalized, there is no need do battle for the resources. Hence the *civilizing role of exchange* (Simmel 1900, pp. 297). In a society based on exchange, maintaining secrecy in order to avoid conflict is less necessary than elsewhere.

g) The autonomy of the exchange act is of supreme importance for the structure of complex systems. Modern systems' theory reminds us that complex systems are not governed from one center, but are decomposed systems. They consist of subsystems, these subsystems in their turn are possibly are comprised of other systems. Subsystems and systems must be *separated from each other by clear boundaries,* the boundaries being the system's self generated elements. Boundaries, according to Luhmann (1984) are among the most important components of complex systems. For one, clearly drawn boundaries enable clear *identification* of the sub-systems, and also the evolvement of clear *environments*. This is equally valid for all complex, i.e. self-organizing systems. In the economy, to delimit, or to draw boundaries means: clear identities of and clear environments (markets). Both emanate from exchange

h) Systems theory designates markets as intraeconomic environment. They are of a quasi parametric nature: the quasi

108

parametric character of markets derives from exchange communication and *only* from exchange communication. Sociologically speaking, the markets obtain the more 'objective' character the more extensively and exclusively communication takes place by way of exchange, and, economically speaking, markets function the better, the finer meshed the net of actual opportunities wherein the transactors act.[6] One can best observe the connection between sociological objectivation and economic functioning in black markets: due to the chance, sporadic and badly organized exchange only a very coarse network can come into being, where price formation is also influenced - constantly varying frictions aside - by personal factors. Therefore price disparities encountered in black markets are large.

Prices thus acquire social objectivity not because of their 'rightness', as being, say, in accordance with a (fictitious) equilibrium or with other criteria as might be applied by an external observer (e.g. W. Pareto), but out of the societal exchange communication. According to Simmel values can be expressed only through exchange. Only through exchange do values obtain a statable amount. We cannot attain another kind of objectivity in economics, as Simmel (1900, pp. 44) points out. To Simmel (and Marx, too) prices are more than mere reflections of scarcities as ratios of quantities (e.g. rates of substitution); they are *embodiments* of social relations which have their own reality. Hence also their relative stability. In consequence, it is unrealistic to expect them to clear markets.

In real economic life the value of a product is determined by the amount of goods or money one can get or one has to pay. The extent of the wedge between these price opportunities can be kept under control only by other exchange opportunities. Beyond exchange there may be (inarticulate) needs and (potential) supplies. But neither any intensity of needs nor supply constraints can contribute to the formation and quantitative determination of values. That means: values are formed and can be formed only in exchange.

According to welfare economics *parametric prices* are essential to safeguarding Pareto-efficient allocation. They are, however, not at all a prerequisite for a proper functioning of the market. Markets are important just where prices are non-parametric (Hayek 1945). Further, the concept of parametric prices - i.e. prices, which the actor cannot influence and to which he will have to adapt his quantities - is useless in our context. So, e.g., State set prices may be parametric *without* contributing to 'objectivating' the economic environment of the enterprise, that is, *to clear boundaries*. For if the State sets a price, it will also have to stand good for the enterprise's losses. Objectivation of prices, then, is a sociological event: it happens by communication between subsystems (agents) acting on their own, independent of the center.

i) In addition, exchange gives enterprises their *goal*: to participate in exchange communication and to build up chances for further participation, that is to earn a profit. Thereby exchange contributes decisively *to the identification of economic organizations*

109

(enterprises) with respect to their surrounding, and to the selfregulation of departments within organizations. On the product markets the enterprise communicates with its environment about price/performance ratios, on the money and capital market about the public's expectations concerning the success of its portfolio management. In that participation in exchange, communication dictates its goal to the enterprise, it becomes largely *independent of personal motives* of managers or owners.

Management might enforce some special style of leadership, e.g. it may exchange long term considerations for short term, but it cannot escape the profit criterion imposed on the firm by exchange communication. Thus exchange communication depersonalizes behaviour of individuals and organizations and renders them more calculable.

From a purely exchange theoretical view organizations (hierarchies) are superfluous: every exchange act is an action out of its own reason. What it is about: to offer a value in order to obtain an other - larger - value. The sense of gathering numerous exchange acts in one organization lies in giving the discontinuous flow of exchange acts a *joint addressee* (firm), and to *mitigate* the technical and attendant financial indivisibilities (indirect costs, overheads) by creating a unified enterprise budget.

Williamson (1981) in his writings on the institutions of capitalism discusses reasons why some economic transactions are preferrably organized by markets and others by hierarchies. Here we are concerned with a more funadamental problem. From what has been said above, follows that *hierarchies are able to operate rationally only if they are imbedded into a market environment.* This means: *only (exchange) communication causes economic agents to behave rationally.* The reader may note that this proposition is in sharp contrast to the traditional economic approach which starts out from making assumptions about the rational individual (homo oeconomicus).

j) Owners, in a modern economy, no longer possess directly physical assets but only of their nominal representations.[7] One can only utilize them (usus fructus and abusus fructus) if exchange communication goes on in society. If it stops, all the owner holds, is printed paper. Exchange communication thus also makes organizations largely independent of owners, thereby increasing the economy's systemic efficiency. Enterprises are more independent, owners are freer.

Hence, in view of systems theory *the most important features of a modern economy* may be summarized as follows:

- socialization in modern economies is performed by exchange;
- mediation of exchange is carried through money as the generalized code for scarcity;[8]
- exchange communication generates economically internal environments for their actual and potential participants,

and at the same time;
- secures their identity despite their overall dependence.

Thus exchange communication generates the formation of clear boundaries between their participants; i.e. *private* or in terms of L.v.Mises (1920), separate *property* (Sondereigentum).

Having emphasized the importance of money for modern civilization, we should make a qualifying remark. It would be fatal, to repeat the mistake of Marxist orthodoxy by inversion, and to assert that market economies would per se be rational. There is no absolute yardstick by which the rationality of a monetized economy could be gauged.[9] What Simmel, Mises and others are suggesting is, that exchange and money - as its embodiment - is responsible for the formal rationality of our economic order without which we never may attain a sensible degree of material welfare (material rationality).[10] There is certainly no alternative to monetized economies. Socialist constructs having assumed the realization of material goals without exchange and money, were doomed to remain utopias. However, we may never expect that monetized economies allowing for economizing on resources are rational from a material point of view since money is completely indifferent to material substance (Simmel 1990, p. 213). Thus market economies interfering with their (natural, mental and social) environment live at the latter's expense since they are largely unable to reflect those costs and reintroduce them into their own respective communication (Luhmann 1988, p. 39). Money does not satisfy wants, but only effective demand. Money economies are blind for certain needs. Besides, money economies produce needs (=problems) which cannot be solved within their competence. Thus money economies are in need of supplementary or complementary communication procedures (politics, state, etc.).

How to orchestrate market coordination in postcommunist Europe?

If exchange is responsible for the maneuverability, efficiency, in a word: high-grade rationality of modern economy, then the question arises, how the exchange communication can be gotten under way in a former command economy. However, when we speak of a kick-off, this cannot mean a new beginning; since a genuine new beginning would presuppose correspondence between communications system and real system; and such correspondence does not exist. The real system is structured as an industrial economy, and the old communications system (non-functional, hence to be supplanted) no longer exists and the new system not yet in existence. Thus the strategists of transformation are faced with the dilemma: where to begin? *On the one hand* exchange presupposes clear boundaries which the system must still generate. Without clear boundaries exchange communication may lead to socially and economically intolerable consequences. As long as the boundaries are not sufficiently clear the state will tend to or will be forced to intervene in the process. *On the other hand* only exchange communication would be capable of generating boundaries (identities and intra-economic environments). Thus there is a snag. Evolution does not get under way: it is threatened with being wrecked by the dilemma of the incongruence between the material and communicative planes.

The question is, who is to communicate on markets and on which markets. Beside households, who, also under the conditions of real socialism, appeared on markets as buyers of goods and sellers of labour, we may distinguish between individual family or group entrepreneurs on the one hand and state enterprises or joint stock companies on the other. While the former communicate only on product markets (by withholding their means of production from valuation by the capital market) the latter must appear also on capital markets.

We shall now examine what possibilities are on offer for getting out of the cul de sac. We shall present several possibilities and then subject them to a critical examination.

1. The possibility of a fresh start on markets for goods and services is present only in the fields of small and *very small entrepreneurial firms and in trade*. Individuals, families, small groups etc. get active as 'simple commodity producers' and they form 'family' enterprises or unincorporated firms. Superficially, support for a petty - bourgeoisie in socialist countries might be considered a relapse into the nineteenth century. But from a system-theoretical view the admission and promotion of private ownership makes sense: true, initially the 'environment' (market) is equally obscure (or as little existing) to them as it is for state enterprises. But small producers of goods or entrepreneur capitalist, as physical persons or their groups are at least unequivocally identifiable actors. Their identity does not derive - as with modern enterprises - only from exchange communication within the system, but from their physical and psycho-social setting. In principle this applies also to group ownership: it should facilitate identification of the group (as a social unit) with the enterprise's functions (as a participant in exchange communication).[11] Even when the exchange system is destroyed, it is easier to initiate exchange communication by means of units that have a natural identity. In addition, the admission of private property has a political and economic meaning. *Politically* it makes sense in that it liberalizes society and that a bourgeois stratum (class) may, in the long run, come into being again. The *economic* significance is the welfare contribution: private ownership can contribute decisively to improving the supply situation if it is not ostracized and thus constantly imperilled in its existence. However,for its contribution to prove really positive, it must grow beyond the function of being able to set up street bazaars: trade must emit positive effects on production.

2. Whereas individuals or groups can more easily begin exchange(s), because they possess at least a psycho-social identity, it is very difficult indeed for exchange to get under way *within the state*

112

sector. This is because socialism of the Soviet stamp rests precisely on the fact that the economy, or 'business', had been replaced by one single economic *organization*. The identity of enterprise(s) was thereby destroyed and the evolution of intra-economy environments (markets) was thwarted, obliterating the boundaries on which the rationality of modern money economies rests. *The transformation consists in the restoration of the boundaries that make possible a clear differentiation of enterprises from their environment*. Reorganization of the large scale public sector is thus the second fundamental task in orchestrating the market a order in Eastern Europe.

In terms of what has been shown above, this can happen only by the *transmutation of bureaucratic into exchange communication*. If communication of state enterprises changed over from bureaucratic to market communication state enterprises would not behave differently from their counterpart in Western countries. For enterprises cannot enter into exchange relations unless they are entitled to possess over their products. Nor can they carry responsibility for the exchange of products if their right to make exchange does not include such rights over investment goods. And finally if the state enterprises' rights are also extended to being entitled to acquire enterprises or portions of enterprises - this being a prerequisite to the coming into existence of capital markets - then that must lead to withdrawal of the state from operative control of the economy. State property like any other property would then also be 'separate' property (Sondereigentum) and the state as economic agent would act as a subject of civil law. The state would in its function as owner be transformed into a large scale capitalist acting through autonomous organizations on markets in managing various assets.

What militates against this prospect is not the systemic logic of a monetized capitalist economy (dominated by the major shareholder, the state), but the difficulty of initiating modern society communications within a socialist economy where there are neither clear enterprise identities, nor clear environments (markets).

While for individual (or group) entrepreneurs at least the identity of the firm is given, thanks to the personal or social identity of its owners, joint stock companies do not enjoy such natural identity. Their identities can be generated only in capital markets. Exchange communication on assets provides the necessary continuity to a firm whose real assets are advanced for a long time. Meanwhile proprietors do enter into short term financial deals. Thus the enterprise becomes largely independent of the very personal interests of proprietors.[12]

Thus we are again confronted with the same dilemma. The evolutionary construction of the communications system may easily evolve from below. After exhibiting successful performance on product markets individual entrepreneur may introduce their assets into the capital market. But once having eradicated the communication how are the giant state enterprises are going to operate simultaneously on product and capital markets? *It is the*

113

simultaneity requirement of product and capital markets that renders the transformation of the etatist economy so difficult.

The formation of product markets in the formerly centrally planning countries is linked to the simultaneous formation of capital markets, because the enterprises can enter the market and act there only under conditions, for which they can also be held responsible. But this does not apply to public enterprises.

- The latter had been furnished by the bureaucracy with certain means of production, whose value determine the enterprises' present indebtedness vis-á-vis the state (or to the commercial banks).
- They were not free in their choice of customer- and supplier relations and further they have often been obliged to fulfil supply functions extraneous to the market.
- In planned economies, enterprise size and organizational forms were determined by considerations extraneous to the market: by the bureaucratic interest to run only a manageable number of large scale units.

For the enterprises these factors make up a structure that has grown under the command economy. It is a structure that is incompatible with market conditions.[13] On the enterprise level, the discrepancy between a historically given and the desired situation in terms of the norms of the market can partly be compensated for a devaluation of its assets. This is the task of the capital market: it must ensure that enterprises operate on the commodity markets under more or less equal chances (Nuti 1989, 27). It must - as also in cases of bankruptcy - be able to enforce corrections in the book value of assets. But their valuation is only possible through acts of exchange, i.e. by all operations that are concerned with their sale or purchase. But concerning profitability, only such actors will be able to communicate with some success, who will thereafter be in a position to organize the potential chances efficiently. Therefore, such actors can be only those who have both sufficient capital and logistic prerequisites to reorganize major firms, furthermore who may market these internationally. Thus it is highly unlikely that Central and Eastern European citizens themselves could dominate this process.

3. The third fundamental measure in orchestrating the market order is the *radical opening* up of the East European economies to the West by abolition of the foreign trade monopoly. A radical opening up of the economy presupposes the convertibility of the currency. The opening vis-á-vis the international product markets provides the economy of East European countries at one stroke with an 'economy-internalenvironment', i.e. the congruity between the internal and external market, whereon the transactors could and must orient themselves. Foreign competition establishes more transparent criteria for the exchange communication between public and private transactors; narrowing their price scope and enforcing quality improvements of output and trade; and thus reducing the power of

the domestic monopolies.

Opening up the economy and formation of the capital market implies *opening up the economies of Eastern Europe to Western capital*. To the latter a *key function* is assigned. In the past and perhaps even now the contribution of Western capital is seen chiefly under the aspect of resource transfer from West to East. True enough, such a contribution is urgently needed in view of the foreign exchange shortage and the enormous need for catching up and for structural change. But even more important is its task with respect to the anticipated transformation, which can only be successfully sustained if the former command economies are transformed into monetized capitalist economies: *because 'capital' is the organizational form of modern economic activity*. Western capital functions as a *heart pacemaker*: it is to set the exchange communication in motion on the level of industrialized countries.

Only an extensive participation of Western capital in new joint stock companies, takeovers of state and other enterprises, joint ventures, founding of new enterprises, can possibly fill the vacuum that came into being by the collapse of the command system. From foreign investments one can expect the following effects:

- Invested Western capital provides the logistics required in industrial economies to master modern technologies and mass production. Important as small and medium sized enterprises in Eastern economies may be, they are not able to perform this particular function. Western investments would function like nerve cells, around which other activities can and will organize themselves. The higher the number of such nodal points, the faster a network of market communications may be generated.
- Western investments will support the transformation process. One of the crucial requirements is that enterprises are autonomous and behave autonomously. After transformation of public firms into joint stock companies the autonomy of enterprises (clear boundaries) can most easily be effected by selling state owned stakes in enterprises to Western corporations. Such privatized or semi-privatized enterprises would really have to function on their own financial responsibility and would therefore become elements of a truly market environment.
- Due to complex logistics that is to be handled by large corporations, Western capital involvement is a sine qua non for the development of capital markets. Since markets are nothing but a network of exchange relations, and exchanges of complex bundles of assets occurs only among partners who are able to organize and economize on these, capital markets will only come into being by the involvement of large Western corporations. The distribution or sale of vouchers or other titles as such will

hardly generate a capital market.

- Involvement of Western capital would also facilitate the participation of the population in privatized enterprises. Without participation of Western capital, vouchers or shares would remain mere printed paper in the hands of Central and Southeast Europe's citizens. It would also be desirable to create 'reverting' constructions, whereby capital invested from the West would flow to an East European fund after a predetermined period.
- Western capital, in particular, if invested by multinational corporations, would support the integration of Central and East European economies into the world economy. Western capital would also counteract the complete disruption of intra-CMEA relations.
- Western investment can support the stabilization measures in Central and Eastern Europe, prevent mass unemployment, ease the process of restructuring reduce shortages, thereby putting a brake on inflation, prevent the traumatic devaluation of the national currencies.

Uneven distribution of chances for transformation among Central and Southeast European nations
Each country has its specific conditions of transformation.
The systemic vacuum is the more menacing

- the higher its economic development level. This is because the discrepancy to be overcome between the complexity of the material structure and that of the system of communication is proportionately greater. At a primitive stage of technological development it is easier for people to find ways of muddling through;
- the more centralized a country was organized the more drastic is the separation of the phases of demolition and of reconstruction; and the more painful are the processes of both demolition and reconstruction;
- the more distorted the material structures are i.e. the more the structures in a Central or Southeast European country differ from those that would have developed under conditions of a market economy;
- the longer the communist rule lasted, the less is the accumulated experience and information concerning market economic institutions and behaviour, and conversely, the more distorted social expectations are.
- The systemic vacuum grows with the cultural distance from the West. Still the help and the degree of penetration to be expected from the West also decreases proportionally to this distance. Cultures once subject to the influence of the Osman empire or of Russian orthodoxy are mostly less Western oriented than those formerly under the influence of the Roman Catholic Habsburgs or of Protestant Prussia. Moreoverthe further

removed in space these countries are, the less will be the relative significance of interchange for their internal development, and the less may they count on Western direct investments.

- Finally, there is the consideration of the factors of macroeconomic conditions such as the degree of indebtedness, the present state of the balance of payments, of excess money supply, rate of inflation and the question of the credibility of economic and transformation policy. However, the discussion of these factors must be left to more competent authors in this volume.

These are some of the aspects, by which the countries' chances for transformation may be evaluated. One may thus assess Hungary's institutional proximity to the Western system as asset per se, which might well counterbalance the burden of that country's relatively high indebtedness. Other countries start off with zero indebtedness; yet their position seems much less favourable.

Now, the more unfavourable the conditions just enumerated, the more likely will a dual economic structure, of bazaar type markets on the one hand and rigid central control structures on the other persist. The more difficult will it be to encourage public enterprises to develop market conform behaviour and to generate the conditions for the emergence of a capital market. And, of course, the more painful will be the opening for a country and the lesser its chances for attracting foreign capital.

Stabilization and systemic change

In Western countries and monetary policies are aimed at perpetuating and stabilizing the economic process, or, to put it in terms of our approach, to assure the likelihood of continuous exchange communication. Since the overall economic activity level is primarily determined by investment decisions, the general setting must be such, as to conform to the expectations of the proprietors of real assets. In order to sustain exchange communication, the domestic and external value of money must be kept as stable as possible. Furthermore there must be a prospect of a sufficient profit rate - either from a high rate of economic growth or due to appropriate restraints on wages. If these conditions are assured, a sufficiently buoyant propensity to invest can be taken for granted.

In principle, the former command economies must also aim at this goal. However, the conditions whereunder this goal may be attained are radically different from those in capitalist countries. As concerns business cycle and monetary policy, reasonably functioning commodity, money and capital markets may be counted on in capitalist countries. Economic policy makers in Central and Southeast Europe are in an infinitely worse position: before they can even given

117

a thought to controlling the overall economic process along the Western example, they must subordinate other economic policy goals to the task of systemic transformation. Unfortunately, cyclical policy measures oriented to growth are normally in contradiction to transformation policy targets. Transformation policy, however, is clearly the primary aim, since without successful transformation any lasting economic development is unthinkable.

Most postsocialist countries are shortage economies because their functioning is not based on exchange communication and they are inadequately monetized. Therefrom two problems devolve: first, money does not buy, or the purchase involves above average transaction costs. That is a restraint on exchange communication. Second, shortage economies lack the price control of competition. Therefore a price liberalization leads to a - possibly self-perpetuating - price explosion. The upsurge of prices may be reduced, if the overall level of demand is restricted and money is kept in short supply. This shows that an economic policy of slowing down the transformation process results in a weakening of economic activity.

While most postsocialist economies are still shortage economy, and therefore show a strong propensity to import, it is desirable in view of their high indebtedness to produce export surpluses. That can only be done by an *appropriately substantial undervaluation of the domestic currency*. Because massive capital imports - and thus a pegging of the exchange rate by capital (in)flows - cannotbe relied upon as long as appropriate systemic conditions have not yet been developed. But in the meantime the Central and Southeast European countries will not be able to produce high rates of growth.

Is it possible to compensate systemic flaws by price discounts?

With the undervaluation of currency we enter upon a subject that deserves some elaboration. Can systemic deficits be compensated by a downwards correction of prices? Prices always represent a compromise, whereby buyer and seller each gain an advantage, whose extent only they are able to assess. But (these) subjective assessments concern not only the actual transaction but also the likelihood of successful follow-up events: what chances does the money (received) promise to the seller, and what chances does the subsequent utilization of the good purchased offer to him as a buyer? To evaluate this, one must come to an assessment on how 'efficient' the 'system' is. If frictions of the system are slight, the seller (buyer) will be content with a lower (higher) price. Frictions may considerably lessen the follow-up likelihoods of exchange transactions.

Prices are to some extent capable of compensating for systemic deficits.[14] Discounts have the function of increasing the likelihood of sales of products in foreign markets, thus bolstering the 'supply forces'.

As typical for Central and Southeast European countries we may cite:

- price discounts vis-á-vis Western goods - specifically for finished goods of otherwise equal quality - to win market

- shares abroad;
- the low market value of fixed assets and current assets and/or the goodwill, even after taking into due consideration the differing productivity, in order to attract foreign capital;
- the same effect is achieved by redistribution of the social product in favour of profits - with dramatic consequences resulting from the drop in real wages;
- on the macroeconomic level, undervaluation of the domestic currency (constituting a deviation from the purchasing power parity level).

Such discounts move, as a rule, by the factors of 2 to 5, in extreme cases even above. Broadly speaking, the larger are needed the discounts the worse the systemic conditions; price discrepancies thus cannot be caught up before the system has been improved.

This connection is also pointed out, int.al., in the literature of Keynesian monetarism (Riese 1990). It is demonstrated there that, in an open economy, the actual opportunities compete for payments: the higher the expected rate of return, the higher the likelihood of an investment (decision). In that competition for money, the effective functioning of the system is of high importance. Similar to the existence of the hierarchy of currencies in monetary Keynesianism (Herr 1989) one may also speak of a hierarchy of systems with respect to their functional capacities.[15] We may thus assume a *yield function*, which relates the rate of profit to the system's degree of functionality: the worse (the better) the system, the higher must (the lower can) be the prospective rate of profit to encourage the economic actors to invest.[16]

We define here the degree of functioning of the 'system' as the

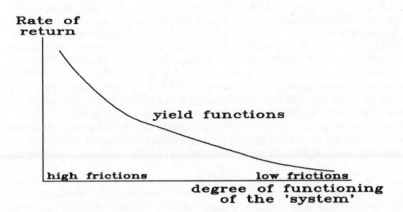

Figure 1 The yield function

inverse of the average degree of frictions the economic agent (entrepreneur) expects to face in the environment he is operating in. Assume that the alternative B is preferable to the existing state A in terms of a rate of return on investment. But substituting B for A entails transaction costs. Then the agent will go from A to B only when the expected costs of transaction (costs of reorganization excluding the direct costs of investments for B) are smaller than the financial benefits he expects. Thus it is not only prices that determine allocation but also frictions that drive a wedge between the respective rates of substitution.

Practical economic men are concerned with the change of the states of affairs rather than with preserving them. In this money performs a central role. Its main contribution is to reduce frictions. In non-monetized economies average frictions may run so high that exchange virtually becomes unattractive: agents would prefer to refrain from exchange. But the 'moneyness' of money is different, as F. Hahn (1982) put it. Money in market economies has a quite higher 'moneyness' as money in ex-socialist countries. First: the set of opportunities to which money relates is much more restricted in postsocialist countries (e.g. to consumer goods and to domestic markets only) than in monetized economies. Second: the average costs of acquiring goods are much higher due to longer search and waiting, and other hazards. The confining of the commodity space and the relatively high frictions of relating opportunities to each other are economic factors which are part of the agents' judgements. The systemic disadvantages are to be compensated by higher profits. This tradeoff is represented by the yield function.

Countries, let us say the USSR or Bulgaria, will have to offer an extremely high rate of return to attract investments, while Hungary, e.g., with lower frictions may be appealing with more modest rates of return. West Germany, on the other extreme, will attract investors with the 'minimum'.

However, the yield function may have a different shape for different trades, as they entail different frictions.

If and when economies are opened, the non-monetary and semi-monetary economies of the Est and the monetized capitalist economies of the West become partners. Of course, *it is the logic of the latter that supplies the yardstick*, by which the value of the formers' economic activities is rated. Preference is given to investment in country A as against investment in country B, if from the point of view of the money owners, the system functions better in country A than in country B. In other words: any malfunctioning such as frictions, shortages or heightened uncertainties is punished by an appropriate deduction in the assessment of the economic earning power.

The yield function implies that the functional differences may be compensated by differences in the return on capital. However, the *compensation potential* appears *limited. Beyond a certain degree of systemic dysfunctionality no price discount, however large* - for product-, asset prices and exchange rates - *and no redistribution*

120

measures, however drastic, could or should compensate for systemic uncertainties and frictions. However, to give an example, there is an exchange rate also for the Soviet rouble where supply and demand would match, but it is way beyond all exchange rates under which a liberal handling of foreign trade might appear rational. In other words: in countries, whose system is still unprepared for a transition to a market economy, *liberalization* of the economy may be undertaken *only step by step.*

The opening may only proceed at a pace that does not lead to a devaluation of all activities or assets, which would practically close the economy again and/or cause such pauperization of the population as to lead to brain drain for that country and a drastic bloodletting. A premature opening can only lead to economic ruin without increasing the chances for the kickoff to exchange communication.

Neoclassic or monetarist inspired therapies often appear to misapprehend these contingencies. Ignoring the systemic circumstances, they recommend a setting of the basic data for achieving an 'equilibrium'. Then, they claim, the market would function. Far from it: after stabilization the economies are still languishing. The market has not yet gotten into stride.

Systemic transformation needs a strong political impulse

From the above it may have become clear that systemic transformation consists in restoring the network of exchange relations, and that the most sensitive part is *how* exchange communication within the state industry can be restarted. In this field massive participation of Western *corporations* seems to be indispensable.

Undoubtedly the countries of Central and Southeast Europe will have to provide the *preconditions* for the start. These are: the elimination of excessive monetary overhang, institution of Western legal and institutional framework: the constitution, civil law, commercial law, the law for joint stock companies, creation of a two tier banking system, a modern tax system (e.g. value added and income taxes) etc. However, *this is only the framework* within which the market will operate, *not the market itself.* The *market as a communicative network can only be started through massive participation of Western capital.* It is the task of Western capital not merely to carry out the function of resource transfer in order to speed up the catching-up process of Central and Southeast Europe; it must also act as a *pacemaker for* the starting-up of the market *system.* It would be quite unrealistic were one to wait for an autonomous upswing. An upturn can come only if Western capital participates intensively in the buildup of Central and Southeast Europe.

Undoubtedly, for Western capital to involve itself, a vigorous political impulse is needed. In free market economies, enterprises desire to remain sole suppliers for as long a time as possible; but entrepreneurs who enter the Eastern scene must hope that many others, too, will engage themselves there. Otherwise than with investments in market sectors where the chances of success diminish with the entry of each additional investor, expectation of success

121

increases with the number of investments entering the Central and Southeast European countries: because the extent and the intensity of participation adds to the system's capacity to function. Thus it is the job of the political actors to diminish threshold anxieties: at this junction the confidence of Western entrepreneurs rests primarily on an assurance that a return to a centrally directed planned economy is highly unlikely. Reliance on and trust in the capacity and ability of the Central and Southeast European countries to build up the market on their own is quite rightly still very weak. And the foreign direct investment extended so far is accordingly small: one wants to have a 'foot in the door', in case of a start-up of a dynamic development - more is not targeted; and that's too little.

If Central and Southeast Europe still has a chance of reintegration into Europe, then the time is now. Never again will the chances be as favourable as now. The Stalinist regimes of Central and Southeast Europe have collapsed, their economies are now still retaining leftovers of their former drive. The systemic vacuum is not yet so old as to drag the economies into complete ruin. It would be quite irresponsible to rest content and wait, or, let us say, to make political and economic stability a condition of Western engagement. Economic stability will not just happen, the social net of the countries of Central and Southeast Europe will collapse, pauperization will continue to advance. And that will be a heavy burden for the young democracies and will fuel the flames of nationalist conflicts. If the West chooses to wait for a miracle, it might find itself forced to erect new walls against the East one day to stem the flood of immigration.

Or does it do so already?

Notes

1. An exception is the essay by Laidler, D. and Rowe, N. (1980), but these authors don't do justice to Simmel.
2. I depart from Luhmann in this point. Luhmann declares *payment* to be the basic act in economy. I follow G. Simmel (1900/1990), who derives his explanation of value and money from *exchange*. There is no direct contradiction to Luhmann, for acts of paying, so far as they ar not unilateral transfers, are acts of exchange.
3. In general equilibrium models agent A does not deal with agent B, D, D etc. before the auctioneer has made his decision.
4. Simmel (1900), and incidentally, also Marx see the origin of money in exchange. 'The value inherent in money it has acquired as a means of exchange; thus where there is nothing to buy, money has no value." (Simmel 1900, p. 134.)
5. Not without reason do systems shift the cause (or source) of wealth from labour (as production factor) or of productivity into the money code and thus into the communicative structure of society (Luhmann 1988, p. 44).
6. Price is also something 'objective' because it manifests itself as a quantity of an 'objective' (=gegenständlich) commodity - in an actual act of barter a good is worth x units of a different good (Marx). Thereby the value expression acquires tangibility. The merchandise, the good representing value, can therefore be used like a commodity. But it is more than just a commodity.
7. By extending exchange communication to enterprises and enterprise parts (stock exchange etc.)

physical assets double into real (physical) assets and financial assets. While enterprises autonomously have disposal over the former, owners - be they natural persons or enterprises - hold the financial assets.

8. The more generalized the money code, the tighter the tie-up between the markets. Only when it is generally used really as a means of exchange, can a *connection of the markets* be effected.

9. On a macroeconomic scale the notion of efficiency is not applicable, says Buchanan (1987, p. 29.)

10. For the distinction between formal and material rationality see Weber (1922, pp. 44.)

11. One of the possibilities of starting exchange communication within the state economy is the transfer of state property to the collective (group). That initially creates group property. This road was taken in Yugoslavia. One tries to create opportunities for the group to identify with the enterprise. But this group does not form a psycho-social unit like a family. It is an economic community of interests, held together by the interest in income. Each of them must therefore have a share in the enterprise: that means distribution of profits (usus fructus) and sales possibilities (abusus fructus). If shares may be handed on (to outsiders), the group property changes quite spontaneously into capitalist private property.

12. In a modern joint stock company virtual everything is substitutable: owners, managers, workers, machines - nonetheless the firm remains.

13. Disparities of market chances are often - not quite correctly - confused with discrepancies in poductivity. Productivity differentials, however, given only an important intimation of differences in market chances. Interesting data concerning productivity differentials between East and West Germany before their unification may be found in (Materialien... 1989). According to data calculated by the German Institute for Economic Research (DIW) the relative East-West productivities varied in some GDR enterprises by between 8% and 80% of the West German branch average. The market would have never tolerated such disparities!

14. This, by the way, applies not only for systemic deficits in the narrow sense but also for all characteristics made responsible by neoclassical theory of market imperfections. But actually it is not a matter of market imperfections, because one cannot hold market forms responsible for goods' characteristics. In this context Carl Menger talks more precisely of graduations in marketability.

15. Differences in interest rates and/or purchasing power parities are a classic example: the less reliable the money, the higher must be the interest rate on the domestic money markets, or the more pronounced must be the undervaluation of the currency concerned.

16. Herr (1989. pp. 106-154) chooses a similar approach to justify international interest and/or purchasing power parity differentials.

Authors

Aslund, Anders is Professor of Economics and Director of the Institute for Soviet and Eastern European Economics at the Stockholm School of Economics. He has published extensively on and in East Europe. His works include two books and countless articles in English. Between 1985-88 Prof. Aslund served as a senior diplomat in the Swedish Embassy in Moscow.

Csaba, László earned his Ph.D. in 1984. Since 1988 he has been Head of the Department for Eastern Europe at KOPINT-DATORG Institute, a large Hungarian business consulting firm. Having served on numerous governmental advisory bodies, since 1990 he has been consultant to the Budapest - based Hungarian-Swedish private investment research firm Centrosearch. Author of 'Eastern Europe in the world economy' (Cambridge U.P., 1990) and over 80 studies published in scholarly journals of 17 countries including the US, Britain, Germany, France, Japan and the Soviet Union.

Dembinski, Paul H. is an international authority on monetary issues as well as on systemic issues of the Eastern European countries. He has widely published on major world languages including several books. Formerly with the University of Geneva since 1990 he has been appointed to Professor of Economics at the University of Fribourg. He is also a partner in the private consulting firm Eco'Diagnostic Analysis in Geneva.

Dietz, Raimund has earned his Ph.D. at the Free University of Berlin in 1974. Since then he's been Senior Fellow at the prestigious Vienna Institute for Comparative Economic Studies. Dr. Dietz has widely published on theoretical and practical aspects of systemic change in

Eastern Europe, on energy economics and East-West relations in Britain, Germany, Hungary, Austria and in the US including the famous green volumes of the Joint Economic Committee of the Congress. His recent research focuses on the theory of money and of systemic transformation. In between 1990-92 Dr. Dietz is a Fellow of the Fritz Thyssen Stiftung, whose support to this study is gratefully acknowledged.

Kolodko, Grzegorz W. is Professor of Economics in the Central School of Planning and Statistics and Director of the Institute of Finance in Warsaw and a member of the economic council of the Polish government. His publications include five books in Polish, and several articles in English, Hungarian Japanese and Italian, among others in the Swiss quarterly Kyklos, in World Development, Economics of Planning and Communist Economies.

Morriset, Jacques has earned his Ph.D. at the University of Geneva. An expert on adjustment policy he is currently associated with the World Bank in Washington.

Oblath, Gábor is chief of International Economic Studies at KOPINT-DATORG Institute in Budapest. His field of research is monetary and exchange rate policy and foreign trade regulation. Having served on various governmental advisory bodies he has published in English pioneering works on the functioning of interstate clearing, including such previously unknown fields as Finnish-Soviet and Hungarian-Soviet practices. A regular consultant to the World Bank, he is author of numerous studies published among others in the Journal of Comparative Economics, Acta Oeconomica and the Forschungsberichte of the Vienna Institute for Comparative Economic Studies.

Roland, Gérard is Professor of Economics at the Université Libre de Bruxelles. His research field is comparative economics. He has done theoretical and applied work on Soviet-type economies. His current research is on the political economy of the transition from plan to market. He has published two books in French and several articles in international economic journals like the European Economic Review, Journal of Comparative Economics, Kyklos, and the Cambridge Journal of Economics.

Szegvári, Iván earned his Ph.D. in Economics at the Bogomolov Institute in Moscow in the year 1982. Since 1984 he's been affiliated with the Institute of Economic Policy and Planning of the Hungarian Ministry of Finance, since 1988 as its Deputy Director. An author of several articles in French, Russian and Hungarian, Dr. Szegvári served on numerous governmental advisory bodies, and is currently a member of the Board of the largest Hungarian commercial bank, MHB.

Subject index

129

Bibliography

Aganbegian, A. (1990): 'Komissiia rekomenduet...' *Ekonomika i Zhizn*, No. 35.

Akerlof, G., (1984): *'An Economic Theorist's Book of Tales'* Cambridge University Press, Cambridge.

Andreff, W. (1989): 'Economic Reforms in North Korea and Viet Nam', *Seoul Journal of Economics*, Vol. 2, No. 1, p. 88-107.

Aslund, A. (1984): 'The Functioning of Private Enterprise in Poland', *Soviet Studies*, no. 3, pp. 427-444.

Aslund, A. (1985): *Private Enterprise in Eastern Europe. The Non-Agricultural Private Sector in Poland and the GDR, 1945-83*, Macmillan, London.

Aslund, A. (1989) *Gorbachev's Struggle for Economic Reform*, Pinter Publishers, London, and Cornell University Press, Ithaca, New York.

Aslund, A. (1990/a): 'Wystarczy 10 holdingów' (Let us start with ten holding companies), *Gazeta Bankowa*, 3 June.

Aslund, A. (1990/b): 'Ctyri pincipy' (Four principles), *Hospodárské noviny*, no. 34.

Aslund, A., (1990/c): *'How to Privatize?'* Stockholm Institute of Soviet and East European Studies, mimeo.

Baecker, D. (1986): *Informationen und Risiko in der Marktwirtschaft*, Dissertation, Univ. Bielefed, Germany.

Bajt, A. (1990): 'Meddig hat Jugoszláviában a sokkterápia?' (How long will the shock therapy last in Yugoslavia?) *Világgazdaság*, 27 April.

Balcerowicz, L. (1991): 'Die "Unreife" der freien Marktwirtschaft in

Polen.' *Neue Zürcher Zeitung*, 13/14 Jan.

Bauer, T. (1984): The Second Economic Reform and Ownership Relations. *Eastern European Economics*, No/1-2/

Blanchard, O. and Layard, R. (1990/a): 'Privatizing Eastern Europe', *Financial Times*, 11 July.

Blanchard, O. and Layard, R., (1990/b): 'Economic Change in Poland', Center for Economic Performance, *Discussion Paper* No 3, May.

Blejer, M. and Khan, M.S. (1984): 'Government Policy and Private Investment in Developing Countries', *IMF Staff Papers*, Vol. 31. No 2.

Blinder, A., (1987): 'Credit Rationing and Effective Supply Failures', *Economic Journal*, Vol. 97. No 2, pp. 327-352.

Bloomestein, H. and Marrese, M. and Zecchini, S, (1991): *'CPEs in Transition: an Introductory Overview of Selected Issues and Strategies'*. In: Bloommestein, H. - Marrese, M. - Zecchini, S. eds.,: op.cit.

Bloomestein, H. and Marrese, M. and Zecchini, S. eds. (1991): *Centrally Planned Economies in Transition*. OECD, Paris

Bokros, L. (1991): Kárpótlás államadósságból. (Restitution from Public Debt). *Magyar Hírlap*, 23 Jan.

Botos, K. (1990): 'A forint konvertibilitásáról' (On convertibility of the forint). *Bankszemle*, No.2.

Brus, W. and Laski, K. (1989): *From Marx to the Market. Socialism in Search of an Economic System*, Clarendon Press, Oxford.

Brus, W., (1975): *Socialist Ownership and Political Systems*, Routledge and Kegan Paul, London

Cagan, P., (1956): 'The Monetary Dynamics of Hyperinflation', in Friedman, M., ed. *Studies in the Quantity Theory of Money*, The University of Chicago Press.

Cairncross, A. (1976): 'The Market and the State', in Wilson, T. and Skinner, A.S. eds: *The Market and the State (Essays in Honour of Adam Smith)*. Oxford University Press, Oxford.

Calvo, G.A. (1983): 'Trying to Stabilize: Some Theoretical Reflections Based on the Case of Argentina', in: Armella, P.A. Dornbusch, R. and Obsfeld, M. (eds.), *Financial Policies and the World Capital Market: The Problem of Latin American Countries*, University of Chicago Press, Chicago.

Ching-yuan, L. (1987): 'Policy Reforms, International Competitiveness and Export Performance: Chile and Argentina Versus the Republic of Korea and Taiwan, Province of China', *IMF Working Paper*, WP/87/49, Washington, D.C., July.

Cicin-Sain, A. (1990): *'Introducing and Maintaining the Convertibility of the Yugoslav Dinar'* - paper presented to the Conference on Economic Cooperation in Europe, Bonn, March 19- April 11.

Csaba, L. (1990/a): *Eastern Europe in the World Economy*. Cambridge University Press.

Csaba, L. (1990/b): The Bumpy Road to the Free Market in Eastern Europe. *Acta Oeconomica*, Vol. 42 No/3-4/

Csaba, L. (1990/c): 'Gearing Up for the Economic Future'. *The New*

Hungarian Quarterly, No 119.

Csaba, L. (1990/d): 'External Implications of Economic Reforms in the European Centrally Planned Economies'. *The Journal of Development Planning*, Vol. 20.

Csaba, L. (1991): 'The Rise and Fall of Comecon.' In: Iivonnen, Y. ed.: *The Soviet Union and the New Europe*. E. Elgar, Aldershot.

Csepi, L., (1991): Vagyonőr, hatóság, gazdálkodó? (A property guard, an authority or entrepreneur?) - an interview to Iván, G. *Magyar Hírlap* 23 Jan.

Dabrowski, M. (1990) 'Trzeba jeszcze wytrac' (We have to hold out) *Polityka*, No. 21.

De Wulf, L. and Goldsbrough, D., (1986): 'The Evolving Role of Monetary Policy in China', *IMF Staff Papers*, No 6, pp. 209-242.

Dembinski, P., (1988): 'Quantity versus Allocation of Money: Monetary Problems of Centrally Planned Economies Reconsidered", *Kyklos*, Vol 41, No 2, pp. 281-300.

Dembinski, P., (1991): *The Logic of the Planned Economy: The Seed of the Collapse*, Oxford University Press, 256 p.

Dewatripont, M. and Roland, G. (1990): 'Economic Reform and Dynamic Political Constraints', mimeo, Université Libre de Bruxelles.

Dhanji, F. and Milanovic B. (1990): *'Privatization in East and Central Europe'* - paper presented at the conference on 'The Transition to a Market Economy in Central and Eastern Europe'. OECD, Paris 28-30 November.

Die CSFR (1991) vor einem langen Weg zur Marktwirtschaft, *Neue Zürcher Zeitung*, 12 Jan, (No 8).

Dietz, R. (1990): 'Reform of Soviet Socialism as a Search for Systemic Rationality'. *Communist Economies*, No.4.

Drach, M., (1986): 'Monnaie et appareil', *Revue d'Etudes Comparatives Est-Ouest*, No 3, pp. 85-96.

Economic Survey of Europe in 1989-1990. United Nations Economic Commission for Europe. New York, 1990.

Edwards, S. (1984): *Stabilization with Liberalization: An Evaluation of Ten Years of Chile's Experiment with Free Market Policies*, 1973-1983, University of California Press, Los Angeles.

Edwards, S., (1989): 'The International Monetary Fund and the Developing Countries: a Critical Evaluation', *Carnegie-Rochester Conference Series on Public Policy*, No 31, pp. 7-68.

Ellman, M. (1989): 'Soviet Economic Reforms: Implementation under Way', paper presented to the NATO colloquium 'Soviet Economic Reforms: Implementation under Way'. Brussels, 22-24 March.

Erhard, L. (1957): *Wohlstand für Alle*, Econ, Düsseldorf.

Feige, E. (1990): 'Perestroika and Socialist Privatization: What is To Be Done? And How?' *Comparative Economic Studies*, No. 3.

Ferge, Zs. (1990): 'The Social Obstacles of Economic Reform in Hungary', *Recherches Economiques de Louvain.*, vol. 56 No 2, pp. 181-190.

Fforde, A. (1990): ' Major Policy Changes and Socio-Economic Development in Vietnam Since mid-1988'. in Ronnas, P. and

Sjöberg, Ö. eds: *Doi Moi: Economic Reforms and Development Policies in Viet Nam.*

Flaeghten, S., (1985): *Monetary Stability in a CPE: the Case of the GDR,* European University Institute, Florence, mimeo.

Franco, G.H.B., (1990): 'Fiscal Reforms and Stabilisation: four Hyperinflation Cases', *Economic Journal,* Vol. 100, No 1, pp. 176-187.

Fry, M., (1988): *Money, Interest, and Banking in Economic Development,* The Johns Hopkins University Press, Washington.

Galbraith, J. K. (1990): 'The Rush to Capitalism', *The New York Review of Books,* 25 October.

Galbraith, J.K. (1952): *A Theory of Price Stabilization,* Harvard University Press, Cambridge.

Gedeon, Sh., (1985/86): 'The Post Keynesian Theory of Money: a Summary and an Eastern European Example.' *Journal of Post Keynesian Economics,* Vol. 8, No 2, pp. 208-221.

Goodman, D.S.G. ed., (1989): 'Zasadnicze pytania' (Fundamental Questions), *Zycie Gospodarcze* No. 42.

Gravy, G., (1977): *Money, Financial Flows and Credit in the Soviet Union,* NBER, Ballinger, Cambridge (Mass).

Gröner, H. and Schüller, A. (1990): 'Supranationalisierung der Wirtschaftspolitik: Funktionswandel internationaler Institutionen?' in: Cassel, D. ed: *Wirtschaftssysteme im Umbruch.* Verlag Vahlen, München, pp. 72-91.

Grosfeld, I. (1990): 'Prospects for Privatization in Poland', *European Economy,* no. 43, pp. 139-150.

Grossman, G., (1966): 'Gold an the Sword: Money in the Soviet Command Economy' in Rosovsky, H., ed, *Industrialization in Two Systems.* J. Wiley, London.

Grossman, S.J. (1976): 'On the Efficiency of Competitive Stockmarkets where Traders Have Diverse Information', *Journal of Finance,* vol. 21 No 2, pp. 573-585.

Grossman, S.J. (1977): 'The Existence of Future Markets, Noisy Rational Expectations and Informational Externalities', *Review of Economic Studies,* vol. 44 no 3, pp. 431-449.

Guitan, M., (1987): 'The Fund's Role in Adjustment', *Finance and Development,* No. 6.

Hahn, F. (1982): *Money and Inflation,* Basil Blackwell, Oxford

Hanson, Ph. (1990): 'Property Rights in the New Phase of Reforms', *Soviet Economy,* no. 2, pp. 95-124.

Hartwig, K-H., and Thieme, J., (1985): 'Determinanten des Geld- und Kreditangebots in sozialistischen Planwirtschaften' in Theime, J., ed, *Geldtheorie: Entwickung, Stand und systemvergleichende Anwendung,* Nomos Verlag, Baden-Baden, pp. 211-235.

Hayek, F. A. (1985/1944): *The Road to Serfdom,* ARK, London.

Hayek, F.A. (1945): 'The Use of Knowledge in Society', *American Economic Review,* Vol. 35. No. 4.

Hayek, F.A. (1988): *The Fatal Conceit: The Errors of Socialism,* The Collected Works of F.A. Hayek, Vol. 1, Routledge, London.

Herr, H. (1989): Weltgeld und die Instabilität der 70er und 80er Jahre.

In: Riese, H. (ed.), *Studien zur Monetaren Theorie, Internationale Geldwirtschaft*, Vol. 2, Transfer Verlag, Regensburg, pp. 106-154.

Hewett, E. (1988): *Reforming the Soviet Economy: Equality versus Efficiency*. The Brookings Institution, Washington D.C.

IMF, IBRD, OECD, EBRD (1990): *The Economy of the USSR*, Washington, DC, 19. December.

Jackson, M. (1990): 'The Privatization Scorecard for Eastern Europe', *RFE-RL Report on Eastern Europe*, 14 December, pp. 23-31.

Jaffee, D.M., and Stiglitz, J. (1988): 'Credit Rationing' in Hahn F.H. and Friedman B., eds: *Handbook of Monetary Economics*, North-Holland, New York etc.

Jasinski, P. (1990): 'Two Models of Privatization in Poland. A Critical Assessment' *Communist Economies*, No. 3.

Kaleta, J. (1990): 'Trzeba calkiem inaczej' (We have to proceed completely otherwise), *Polityka*, No. 6.

Karpinski, A. (1989): 'Prognozowanie - programowanie - planowanie' (Forecasting - Programming - Planning), *Gospodarka Planowa*, No. 3, p. 23-29.

Kaser, M. (1987): 'One Economy, two Systems: Parallels Between Soviet and Chinese Reforms'. *International Affairs*, (London) No.3.

Kawalec, S. (1989): 'Privatization of the Polish Economy', *Communist Economies*, No. 3.

Kawalec, S. (1990): 'Employee Ownership, State Treasury Ownership: Dubious Solutions', *Communist Economies*, No. 1.

Khan, M.S., and Montiel P., (1989): 'Growth-Oriented Adjustment Programs: a Conceptual Framework', *IMF Staff Papers*, vol. 36, No. 2.

Khan, M.S., Montiel, P., and Haque, N.U., (1990): 'Adjustment with Growth', *Journal of Development Economics*, Vol. 32, No. 2, pp. 155-179.

Kivilathi, T. and Rantava, J. (1990): 'New Framework for Trade between Finland and the Soviet Union', *Bank of Finland Bulletin*, December.

Klaus, V. (1990): 'Policy Stances of CPEs That Are Not in the IMF World Bank Toward Those Organizations.' *Soviet and Eastern European Foreign Trade*, Vol. 26. No 2.

Kolodko G. W. (1991): 'Polish Hyperinflation and Stabilization 1989-1990'. *MOST - Economic Journal on Eastern Europe and The Soviet Union* (Bologna) No. 1. pp. 9-36.

Kolodko, G.W. (1987): *Polska w swiecie inflacji* (Poland in the World of Inflation), Ksiazka i Wiedza, Warsaw.

Kolodko, G.W. (1988): 'Economic Change and Shortageflation Under Centrally Planned Economies', *Economia delle Scelte Publiche* No. 1 p. 15-32.

Kolodko, G.W. (1989b): 'Proby stabilizacji' (Trying to Stabilize), *Wektory Gospodarki*, No. 5, p. 2-5.

Kolodko, G.W. (1989c): 'Kierunki dzialan stabilizacyjnych'. (The Directions of Stabilizing Action), *Finanse*, No. 7-8.

Kolodko, G.W., and McMahon, W.W. (1987): 'Stagflation and

Shortageflation: A Comparative Approach', *Kyklos*, No. 2, p. 176-197.

KOPINT-DATORG (1990): *'Economic Trends in Eastern Europe and the World Economy'*, Autumn.

Kornai J. (1990/b): 'Kiegészítések a "Röpirathoz"', (Further thoughts on The Road...") *Közgazdasági Szemle*, No. 7-8.

Kornai, J. (1980): *Economics of Shortage*, North Holland, Amsterdam.

Kornai, J. (1984): 'Bureaucratic and Market Coordination'. *Osteuropa Wirtschaft*, No 4.

Kornai, J. (1986): 'The Hungarian Reform Process: Visions, Hopes, and Reality', *Journal of Economic Literature*, No. 4.

Kornai, J. (1988): 'Individual Freedom and Reform of the Socialist Economy', *European Economic Review*, vol. 32, No. 2-3, pp. 233-268.

Kornai, J. (1990/a) *The Road to a Free Economy. Shifting from a Socialist System: The Example of Hungary*, Norton, New York, and London.

Kornai, J. (1990/c): 'The Affinity Between Ownership and Coordination Mechanisms'. In: Bogomolov, O. ed. (1990): *Market Forces in Planned Economies*, MacMillan, London-Basingstoke, pp. 32-54.

Kosai, Y. (1986): *The Era of High-Speed Growth. Notes on the Postwar Japanese Economy*, University of Tokyo Press, Tokyo.

Köves, A. (1983): 'Implicit Subsidies and Some Issues of Economic Relations within the CMEA'. *Acta Oeconomica*, No.1-2.

Köves, A. (1991): 'Transforming Commercial Relations within the CMEA: the Case of Hungary'. In: Köves, A. and Marer, P. eds. (1991): op.cit.

Köves, A. and Marer, P. eds. (1991): *Foreign Economic Liberalization: Transformations in Socialist and Market Economies*. Westview Press, Boulder, Colorado.

Köves, A. and Oblath, G. (1989): 'Foreign Economic Strategy and Policy Reform in Hungary'. Bacground paper prepared for the Blue Ribbon Commission. Budapest.

Laidler, D. and Rowe, N. (1980): 'Simmel's Philosophy of Money - A Review Article for Economists', *Journal of Economic Literature*, Vol. 18. No. 1, pp. 97-105.

Lányi, K. (1990): 'Is It Really Dangerous to Trade in Dollars with the Soviet Union?' *Acta Oeconomica*, Vol. 42. No. (3-4).

Lavoie, D. (1985): *Rivalry and Central Planning. The Socialist Calculation Debate Reconsidered*, Cambridge University Press, Cambridge.

Lavoie, M., (1984): 'The Endogenous Flow of Credit and the Post Keynesian Theory of Money', *Journal of Economic Issues*, Vol. 18, No.3, pp. 771-797.

Leff, N., and Sato, K. (1980): 'Macroeconomic Adjustment in Developing Countries: Instability, Short-Run Growth and External Dependency', *Review of Economics and Statistics*, Vol. 62, No. 2.

Lewandowski, J. and Szomburg, J. (1989): 'Property Reform as a Basis for Social and Economic Reform', *Communist Economies*, No. 3.

136

Linder, W. (1990): 'Dritter Weg - reale Alternative oder semantische Spilerei?' *Europäische Rundschau*, No. 2.

Lipton, D. and Sachs, J. (1990): 'Creating a Market in Eastern Europe: The Case of Poland', *Brookings Papers on Economic Activity*, No. 1.

Luhmann, N. (1988): *Die Wirtschaft der Gesellschaft*, Frankfurt a.M., Suhrkamp.

M.Zs. (1990): 'Befagyasztják a jugoszláv devizaszámlákat'. (Yugoslav foreign currency accounts are being frozen). *Világgazdaság*, 22 December.

Machinea, J.L. and Fanelli, J.M. (1989): 'Stopping Hyperinflation: The Case of the Austral Plan in Argentina, 1985-87', in: M. Bruno, D. Di Tella, R. Dornbusch and S. Fisher, eds. *Inflation Stabilization. The Experience of Israel, Argentina, Brazil, Bolivia and Mexico.* The MIT Press, Cambridge.

Markovic, A. (1990): 'Az egész ország programja' (The Program of the Whole Country). *Magyar Szó*, 26 July.

Marrese, M. and Vanous, J. (1983): *Soviet Subsidization of Trade with Eastern Europe: A Soviet Perspective.* Berkley, Institute of International Studies, University of California.

Materialien (1989) zu Bericht zur Lage der Nation. Bundesministerium für Innendeutsche Beziehungen, Bonn, 1989. - mimeo.

McKinnon, R. I., (1990): 'Stabilizing the Ruble', *Communist Economies*, No. 2.

Millar, J. R. (1990): 'Perestroika and Socialist Privatization: What is To Be Done? A Comment: There Is No Quick Fix.' *Comparative Economic Studies*, No. 3.

Mises, L. (1920): 'Die Wirtschaftsrechnung im sozialistischen Gemeinwesen', *Archiv für Socialpolitik*, Vol. 47, S. 86-121.

Mises, L. von (1972/1920): 'Economic Calculation in the Socialist Commonwealth' in Nove, A. and Nuti M., eds. *Socialist Economics*, Penguin, Harmondsworth, pp. 75-91.

Mizsei, K. (1990): 'Shock or Therapy? Poland, Yugoslavia, Hungary.' *The New Hungarian Quarterly*, No. 119.

Molnár Zs. (1990): 'Kómában a jugoszláv gazdaság' (The Agony of the Yugoslav Economy). *Világgazdaság*, 14 August, 1990.

Morisset, J., (1990): '*Is Financial Liberalization in LDCs Really Favorable to Private Investment?*', Department of Political Economy of the University of Geneva, mimeo.

Murrell, P. (1990): 'Big Bang' versus Evolution: East European Economic Reforms in the Light of Recent Economic History', *PlanEcon Report*, 29 June.

Newbery, D. (1991): 'Reform in Hungary: Sequencing and Privatisation', *European Economic Review*, (forthcoming).

North, D. C. (1981): *Structure and Change in Economic History*, Norton, New York and London.

Nuti, D. (1988): '*Perestroika*: the Economics of Transition Between Central Planning and Market Socialism', Paper presented to the Conference on Plan and/or Market at the Institut für die

Wissenschaften vom Menschen, Vienna, 15-18 Dec.

Nuti, D.M. (1982): 'The Polish Crisis: Economic Factors and Constraints.' In: Drewnowski J. ed., *Crisis in East European Economy. The Spread of Polish Disease*, Croom Helm, London-Canberra, St. Martin's Press, New York.

Nuti, M. (1991): '*Privatisation of Socialist Economies: General Issues and the Polish Case*.' In: Blommestein, H. and Marrese, M. and Zecchini, S. eds., op. cit.

Nuti, M., (1985): 'Hidden and repressed inflation in Soviet-type economies: definitions, measurements and stabilization', *Contributions to Political Economy*, No. 5, pp. 3-49.

Nuti, M., (1987): Financial Innovation under Market Socialism, European University Institute, Florence, *Working Papers*, No. 285.

Oblath, G. (1990): 'Hungary's debt burden and the need for Western assistance', mimeo. KOPINT-DATORG, Budapest.

Oblath, G. and Tarr, O. (1991): 'The Soviet "Subsidization" of Eastern Europe: The Case of Hungary'. *World Bank Discussion Papers*, forthcoming.

Oblath, G. and Pete, P. (1985): 'Trade with the Soviet Union: the Finnish Case'. Acta Oeconomica, Vol. 35 (1-2), pp. 165-194.

Okolicsanyi, K. (1990): 'Privatization: Two Cautious Steps', *RFE-RL Report on Eastern Europe*, 19 October.

Olson, M. (1965): *The Logic of Collective Action*, Harvard University Press, Cambridge (Massachusetts).

Orléan, A. (1990): 'Contagion mimétique et bulles spéculatives', in Cartelier, J. ed. *La formation des grandeurs économiques*, Presses Universitaires de France.

Pajestka, J. (1989): *Prolegomena globalnej racjonalnosci czlowieka*. (Prolegomenon of Overall Human Rationality), Institut of Economics of the Polish Academy of Sciences, Warsaw.

Pelikan, P. (1990): 'Evolution of Structures, Schumpeter Efficiency, and a Limit to Socialist Economic Reforms', *Working Paper* no. 2, Stockholm Institute of Soviet and East European Economics.

Perekhod (1990) k rynku. Konstseptsiya i progra:nma, Moscow, August.

Pipes, R., (1990): 'Gorbachev's Russia: Breakdown or Crackdown?' *Commentary*, Vol 89 No 3 pp. 13-25.

Podolski, T., (1986): *Financial Innovation and the Money Supply*, Oxford, Basil Blackwell.

Podolski, T.M., (1987): *Socialist Banking and Monetary Control: the Experience of Poland*, Cambridge University Press, Britain.

Polak, J.J. (1989): 'Politiques financiéres et developpement', *Etudes du Centre de Développement*, OECD, Paris.

Portes, R., (1983): 'Central Planning and Monetarism: Fellow Travelers?' in Desai, P., ed. *Marxism, Central Planning and the Soviet Economy*, MIT Press, Cambridge, Mass. pp. 149-165.

Pravitelstvennaia programma (1990) formirovaniia struktury i mekhanizma reguliruemoi rynochnoi ekonomiki, Moscow, September.

Program (1983): 'Rzadowy program przeciwdzialania inflacji'

(Governmental Anti-Inflationary *Program*), *Trybuna Ludu,* 24 March.

Program (1989): 'Zarys programu gospodarczego Rzadu' (An Outline of Governmental Economic Program), *Rzeczpospolita,* 12 October.

Propozycje (1989) przeksztalcen polskiej gospodarki, (A proposal to transform the Polish Economy) Zesztyty Naukowe PTE, Warsaw.

Pulai, M. ed. (1989): *'A forint konvertibilitásáról. Kormányzat és gazdaság. Az antiinflációs gazdaságpolitika lehetőségéről'.* (On Convertibility of the Forint. The State and the Economy. Possibilities for Antiinflationary Policies), Budapest, Közgazdasági és Jogi Könyvkiadó.

Ramos, J.R. (1980): 'The Economics of Hyperstagflation: Stabilization Policy in Post-1973 Chile', *Journal of Development Economics,* No. 7.

Riese, H. (1990): *Geld im Sozialismus - Zur theoretischen Fundierung von Konzeptionen des Sozialismus,* Transfer-Verlag, Regensburg.

Roca, S.G. (1989): *Socialist Cuba. Past Interpretations and Future Challenges,* Westview Press, Boulder & London.

Rockoff, H. (1984): *Drastic Measures. A History of Wage and Price Controls in the U.S.,* Cambridge University Press, Cambridge.

Roland, G. (1989a): *Économie politique du systéme soviétique,* L'Harmattan, Paris.

Roland, G. (1989b): 'Régulation et réforme en URSS', *Revue d'Etudes Comparatives Est-Ouest,* vol. 20 No 3, pp. 39-70.

Roland, G. (1990a): 'Introducing the Market in a Shortage Economy: Introducing the Vertical Integration Issue', *Recherches Economiques de Louvain,* vol. 56 No 2, pp. 221-238.

Roland, G. (1990b): 'Vers une zone ECU en Europe de l'Est?', *De Pecunia,* vol. 11 No 2-3, pp. 553-564.

Roland, G. (1990c): 'On the Meaning of Aggregate Excess Supply and Demand for Consumer Goods in Soviet-Type Economies', *Cambridge Journal of Economics,* vol. 14 No 1, pp. 49-62.

Rosenberg, N. and Birdzell, L.E. (1986): *How the West Grew Rich,* Basic Books, New York.

Rostowski, J., (1989): 'Stopping Very Rapid Inflation under Capitalism: the Implications for Reformed Communist Economies', London, mimeo.

Rostowski, J. (1990): 'The Decay of Socialism and the Growth of Private Enterprise in Poland' in Gomulka, S., and Polonsky A. eds., *Polish Paradoxes,* Routledge, London and New York, pp. 198-223.

Sachs, J. (1990): 'What is to be done? *The Economist,* 13 January.

Sargent, T., (1982): 'The End of Four Big Inflations', In Hall, R. (ed) *Inflation: Causes and Effects,* Chicago, NBER and Chicago University Press, 1982.

Schrettl, W. (1991): *'Structural Conditions for a Stable Monetary Regime and Efficient Allocation of Investment: Soviet Union Country Study'.* In: Blommestein, H., Marrese, M. and Zecchini, S. eds., op. cit.

Siebert, H. (1990): 'The Economic Consequences of German Unification.' *Kieler Diskussionsbeiträge*, No. 160/a - September.

Simmel, G. (1990/1900): *The Philosophy of Money*, Routledge, London.

Soós, K. A. (1986): *Terv, kampány, pénz* (Plan, Campaigns, Money). Közgazdasági és Jogi Könyvkiadó, Budapest

Soós, K. A. (1990): 'Sokkterápia vagy gazdaságpolitikai fordulat?' (Shock therapy or a turn in economic policy?) *Magyar Hírlap*, 24 August.

Stiglitz, J., (1988): 'Money, Credit, and Business Fluctuations', *Economic Record*, No. 4.

Szamuely, L. ed. (1989): 'Opening Towards the World Economy - a Turn in Economic Policy'. *The Hungarian Economy*. Vol. 17. No. 1.

Szegvári, I. (1990): 'Külkereskedelmi irányítás és a szocialista országok reformfolyamata'. (Foreign Trade Regulation and the Reform Process in Socialist Countries). *Gazdaság*, No. 4.

Szép, I. (1990) 'Hogyan lesz a 300 milliárdból még több?' (How will 300 bn grow further?) *Világgazdaság*, 6 Sept.

Szymkiewicz, K. (1988): 'Le commerce extérieure: "Locomotive" de la reforme économique'. *Le Courrier des pays de l'Est*, Sept.

Tanzi, V. (1977): 'Inflation, Lags in Collection and the Real Value of Tax Revenue', *IMF Staff Papers*, Number 1.

The World Bank (1991): 'The Demise of the CMEA: Implications for Hungary'. Document of the World Bank.

Topinski, A. (1989): Nierownowage rynku a przedsiebiorstwa, (Market disequilibria and the firms) *Gospodarka Planowa*, No. 3, p. 29-36.

Traimond, P., (1979): *Le rouble: monnaie passive et monnaie active*, Cujas, Paris.

Triska, D.(1990): *'Privatization in Post-Communist Czechoslovakia'*, paper presented at the conference 'In Search of the Capitalist', Stockholm, 3 October.

Van Wijnbergen, S., (1983): 'Credit Policy, Inflation and Growth in a Financially Repressed Economy', *Journal of Development Economics*, Vol. 13, No. 1. pp. 45-65.

Vanous, J. (1989): 'Privatization in Eastern Europe: Possibilities, Problems, and the Role of Western Capital', *PlanEcon Report*, 30 September.

Várhegyi, É. (1990): Pénzfolyamatok - a kormányzati törekvések ellenében (Financial processes - counteracting governmental decisions). *Külgazdaság*, No.8.

Wasilewski, T. (1990): *'Exchange Rate Policy in the Transition to the Market Economy in Poland'* - paper presented to the EACES conference, Verona, 27-29 September.

Wiles, P. (1977): *Economic Institutions Compared*, Basil Blackwell, Oxford.

Williamson, O.E. (1981): 'The Economics of Organization', *American Journal of Sociology*, Vol. 87, No. 3, pp. 548-577.

Winiecki, J. (1988): *The Distorted World of Soviet-Type Economies*,

Oxford.

Williamson, O.E. (1981): 'The Economics of Organization', *American Journal of Sociology*, Vol. 87, No. 3, pp. 548-577.

Winiecki, J. (1988): *The Distorted World of Soviet-Type Economies*, Routledge, London etc.

Winiecki, J. (1990): 'Post-Soviet-Type Economies in Transition: What Have We Learned from the Polish Transition Programme in Its First Year?' *Weltwirtschaftliches Archiv*, Vol. 126, No 4.

Yakutin, Y. (1990): 'Alternativa rinku - a est' li ona?' *Ekonomika i Zhizn*, No. 35.

Zwass, A., (1978): *Money, Banking and Credit in the Soviet Union and in Eastern Europe*, Macmillan, London.